# Retire Boldly

## Position Yourself to Champion Your Ambitions

Russell W. Strickler, CFP®, AIF®
Strickler Financial Group

Copyright © 2025 by Russell W. Strickler and Advisors Excel, LLC.

All rights reserved. No part of this publication may be reproduced, distributed, or transmitted in any form or by any means, including photocopying, recording, or other electronic or mechanical methods, without the prior written permission of the publisher, except in the case of brief quotations embodied in critical reviews and certain other noncommercial uses permitted by copyright law. For permission requests, write to the publisher at the address below. These materials are provided to you by Russell W. Strickler for informational purposes only and Russell W. Strickler and Advisors Excel, LLC expressly disclaim any and all liability arising out of or relating to your use of same. The provision of these materials does not constitute legal or investment advice and does not establish an attorney-client relationship between you and Russell W. Strickler. No tax advice is contained in these materials. You are solely responsible for ensuring the accuracy and completeness of all materials as well as the compliance, validity, and enforceability of all materials under any applicable law. The advice and strategies found within may not be suitable for every situation. You are expressly advised to consult with a qualified attorney or other professional in making any such determination and to determine your legal or financial needs. No warranty of any kind, implied, expressed, or statutory, including but not limited to the warranties of title and non-infringement of third-party rights, is given with respect to this publication.

Russell W. Strickler /Strickler Financial Group
10299 E. Grand River Rd. Suite I Brighton MI 48116
www.stricklerfinancial.com

Book layout ©2022 Advisors Excel, LLC
Retire Boldly/Russell W. Strickler. — 2nd edition
ISBN 9798300515317

Russell W. Strickler is registered as an Investment Advisor Representative and is a licensed insurance agent in the states of Michigan Ohio, and Florida. Strickler Financial Group is an independent financial services firm that helps individuals create retirement strategies using a variety of investment and insurance products to custom suit their needs and objectives.

Investment advisory products and services made available through AE Wealth Management, LLC (AEWM), a Registered Investment Adviser. Strickler Investment Services, LLC is a registered investment advisor. Russell Strickler is the managing member and investment advisor representative of the firm.

Insurance products are offered through the insurance business Strickler Financial Group. Strickler Financial Group is also an Investment Advisory practice that offers products and services through Strickler Investment Services, LLC, a Registered Investment Advisor. The insurance products offered by Strickler Financial Group are not subject to investment Advisor requirements.

Certified Financial Planner Board of Standards, Inc. (CFP Board) owns the certification marks CFP®, CERTIFIED FINANCIAL PLANNER™, and CFP® (with plaque design) in the U.S., which it authorizes use of by individuals who successfully complete CFP Board's initial and ongoing certification requirements.

The Accredited Investment Fiduciary (AIF®) Designation demonstrates the individual has met educational standards to carry out a fiduciary standard of care and acting in a client's best interest.

The contents of this book are provided for informational purposes only and are not intended to serve as the basis for any financial decisions. Any tax, legal, or estate planning information is general in nature. Please remember that converting an employer plan account to a Roth IRA is a taxable event. Increased taxable income from the Roth IRA conversion may have several consequences. Be sure to consult with a qualified tax advisor before making any decisions regarding your IRA. It should not be construed as legal or tax advice. Always consult an attorney or tax professional regarding the applicability of this information to your unique situation.

Information presented is believed to be factual and up-to-date, but we do not guarantee its accuracy, and it should not be regarded as a complete analysis of subjects discussed. All expressions of opinion are those of the author as of the date of publication and are subject to change. Content should not be construed as personalized investment advice, nor should it be interpreted as an offer to buy or sell any securities mentioned. A financial advisor should be consulted before implementing any strategies presented.

Investing involves risk, including the potential loss of principal. No investment strategy can guarantee a profit or protect against loss in periods of declining values. Any references to protection benefits or guaranteed/lifetime income streams refer only to fixed insurance products, not securities or investment products. Insurance and annuity product guarantees are backed by the financial strength and claims-paying ability of the issuing insurance company. Strickler Financial Group is not affiliated with the U.S. government or any governmental agency.

*Any names used in the examples in this book are hypothetical only and do not represent actual clients.*

*"All you need is the plan, the road map, and the courage to press on to your destination."*
***~ Earl Nightingale***

*This book is dedicated to:*

*My wife Sarah — for being my better half and always having the faith in me during my pursuits, no matter how crazy they may seem at the time.*

*My parents, Tony and Kathy — for not giving me everything I wanted, but for giving me everything I needed.*

*Coach Decker —for teaching me so much more than just basketball. (Although, I may still throw up thinking about those 60-second sprinting drills.)*

# Table of Contents

PREFACE

# Dare to Retire Boldly

Not everyone can say they graduated from Yale. I can, but some clarification is necessary.

Yale is the small community where I grew up in Michigan, north of Detroit and some thirty miles west of Lake Huron. Before graduating from Yale, umm, High School, I became well aware of every little aspect, including the town's unofficial title as Bologna Capital of the World, in part because my mom worked at the town grocery store, and still does.

If I really wanted to embellish my stature as a Yale graduate, I could emphasize, "That's no baloney," and have a field day with my heritage.

The thing is, my upbringing wasn't anything special. I loved sports, and at 6-foot-5, I could excel among opponents we faced from other small schools. Yet those opportunities left me wondering about how I could have stacked up playing football, basketball, and baseball at a high school with a larger enrollment. Could I have attracted any recruiting attention from college coaches, much like my nephew, who has made the most of the opportunities he gained from playing at that level.

I grew jealous of friends who participated on travel teams or could buy cool new releases of video games. My parents worked hard, though, and while they may not have furnished everything I wanted, I received everything I needed.

The perspective I gained from that upbringing inspires me every day. I want my clients to embrace their retirement to-do list and maximize their opportunities. Much like I would dream boldly about different athletic pursuits, I want clients to Retire Boldly.

You retire only once. It is imperative you get it right.

That means accessing the funds you accumulated over many years. You likely made sacrifices during your work career — resisting the urge to take an exotic vacation, or perfect your ability to tame the slopes, or enjoy a cabin getaway while limiting out on walleye.

Perhaps your ambitions are even bolder. An African safari or a tour of the Holy Land might be your ultimate travel destination. If so, don't rule out anything just because you decided against it while working — especially if it involves what many consider the ultimate retirement preference: spending time with grandkids.

Retirement requires a new approach and mindset. You want to be active, especially during your early retirement years, because you will then have the health and stamina to attack your bucket list.

The difference between steadfastly building your savings and spending your savings is contradictory. Sometimes, it almost seems foreign to spend a little (or especially spend a lot) after caretaking your portfolio for three or four decades. Again, it's a mindset reversal and a key component behind being able to Retire Boldly.

Affirming your ability to spend money in retirement requires confidence. That is why a comprehensive and viable retirement plan, which can always be tweaked to accommodate life's unexpected events, is vital. Remember the television commercials advocating that you find your "retirement number" representing the amount you need to save?

Those ads never seemed to establish the purpose of the messaging. What does your pile of retirement savings mean to you? What is it for?

Important questions, really. When constructing a retirement income plan, a financial advisor should strive to understand what makes you tick. That means asking additional questions to get to know you and your desires. Sure, the plan must account for contingencies that can impact your resources, such as taxes, inflation, and health care. Yet it also must incorporate an additional step that accounts for your goals — a retirement action plan, if you will.

Some in the financial industry do not incorporate this additional step. They focus on investments and growing your money, which is great while you're making a steady paycheck.

Retirement, however, is about funding your lifestyle without the income you relied on during your work career. Maintaining your lifestyle is vital. It reflects who you are and what you enjoy. Why curtail those pleasures only to worry whether your portfolio meets your expectations?

Quite possibly, it's because you don't have a financial advisor at your side to champion your aspirations and provide thumbs-up encouragement to enjoy pursuits that had once merely been retirement dreams.

That's where our Retire Boldly team can step in and assist, Even among retirement planners, consumers often navigate a sea of sameness when examining different financial advisors.

I like to inject the phrase, YOLO, when speaking with people who visit our firm. The acronym stands for "you only live once."

To reiterate, we all must realize retirement better be right because you've got only one shot at constructing a viable plan. Yet once we carefully analyze the details regarding that plan, it often frees opportunities to unlock your retirement ambitions. Retirees find it liberating to let go of the natural inclination to hold on to retirement savings because they may do something wrong and be unable to pay their bills in the future.

A potential bonus exists to the analysis we conduct. For pre-retirees, our findings can sometimes reveal the possibility of being able to retire earlier than anticipated.

My aunt happened to be my first client. She is the youngest of my mother's siblings. After reviewing her financial outlook and also discussing her retirement vision, I informed her she could retire. She was then in her early fifties and didn't seem inclined to retire just yet.

Until one day, I received a text from her out of the blue. Short and sweet, she wrote, "I'm retired." Taken aback, I reached out, and she confirmed the monumental decision, which she confined to a modest message.

Suddenly, the "now what?" phase became reality, but through our discussions, my aunt had an income plan and an action plan. One of the greatest attributes to that is it's not always about the places you go or people you see. You can begin forging your legacy while you're still alive.

Gifting with a warm hand rather than a cold one can be as fulfilling as anything you achieve in retirement. Getting to enjoy the pleasure others gain from your love and benevolence is another purposeful facet of being able to Retire Boldly.

Retirement confidence escalates knowing that potentially threatening elements, such as taxation, inflation, and health care, can be mitigated with proper planning.

Fulfilling your desired lifestyle can embolden that confidence after realizing a Retire Boldly plan is not only about preserving your assets but also pursuing your ambitions.

# Potential Risks to Your Ideal Retirement

Ever feel like life gets in the way and prevents you from doing things you shouldn't ignore? I think if we're honest with ourselves, we've all put off obligations we know are important. In your case, you may be reading this book because it's time to get serious about financial planning and, specifically, devising a way to ideally prepare for retirement. A retirement plan should be based on more components than just your investments or your finances. The preparation of that strategy begins with your desires, ambitions, and goals for this fulfilling season of life.

There's no such thing as a silly question — not when one of the most common questions we hear from folks regarding retirement is, "Am I going to be okay?" It often seems people are reluctant to meet with financial professionals because they worry they might sound uneducated. However, it's understandable for you to be a novice when it comes to financial issues and retirement concerns. You've been busy with your lives and your careers. Time spent away from work has meant time spent being around those you love and engaging in the activities you enjoy. Retirement provides the opportunity to do even more of that while not fretting over work obligations.

Concerns people have about what they may encounter during retirement can be far-reaching and still perfectly legitimate. For a quick snapshot, I want to provide a brief sampling of wide-ranging issues that can come up during discussions about what to potentially brace for in retirement. This book will touch on many of these issues in further detail.

**Politics:** A presidential election often stirs emotions regarding potential effects on the economy. Investors grow anxious about how a new president can influence market returns. It's Congress, however, that establishes tax laws and passes spending bills. Yet the president can indirectly affect the economy and the stock market in various ways such as the appointment of policymakers, development of international relations, and influential sway on new legislation.

**Taxes:** An example of a president's influence can be cited in signature legislation passed during Donald Trump's presidency, the Tax Cuts and Jobs Act of 2017. However, our tax system remains progressive, so the more you earn, the higher the tax rate within each tax bracket of subsequently higher income. A thorough understanding of tax regulations can be crucial. A financial professional can help identify potential issues a tax professional can help solve.

**Inflation:** General increases in the prices of goods and services, often measured using the consumer price index (CPI), can stem from fluctuations in real demand for goods and services. Inflation can discourage investment, as well as shortages in goods. A retiree's income can be impacted by the effect inflation can have on a fixed budget. The value of currency decreases because inflation erodes purchasing power.

**Cybersecurity:** Think you'll give up your smartphone in retirement? No way, right? It's here to stay, along with other intellectual gadgetry, including devices that have not been patented or invented yet. Retirees are becoming more tech-savvy, yet they can also be more trusting, which can be problematic when responding to potential scammers by phone, text, or email. Cybercrime often uses technology to target potential victims. Scammers, much like technology, will likely only grow more sophisticated over time.

CHAPTER 1

# Longevity

You would think the prospect of the grave would loom more frightening as we age, yet many retirees say their number one concern is actually running out of money in their twilight years.[1] Unfortunately, this concern is justified because of one significant factor: We're living longer.

According to the Social Security Administration's 2011 Trustee Report, in 1950, the average life expectancy for a sixty-five-year-old man was seventy-eight, and the average for a sixty-five-year-old woman was eighty-one.[2] In the 2023 Trustees Report issued by the SSA, those averages were eighty-three and eighty-six, respectively.[3]

The bottom line of many retirees' budget woes comes down to this: They just didn't plan to live so long. Now, when we are younger and in our working years, that's not something we necessarily see as a bad thing; don't some people fantasize about living forever or, at least, reaching the ripe old age of 100?

However, with a longer lifespan, we face a few snags as we retire. Our resources are finite — we only have so much money

---

[1] Brett Arends. MarketWatch. June 5, 2023. "Americans are 'more afraid of running out of money than death'" https://www.marketwatch.com/story/americans-are-more-afraid-of-running-out-money-than-death-ee5e22e9

[2] Social Security Administration. 2024. "Actuarial Publications: Cohort Life Expectancy" https://www.ssa.gov/oact/TR/2011/lr5a4.html

[3] Social Security Administration. 2023. "Period Life Expectancy — 2023 OASDI Trustees Report" https://www.ssa.gov/OACT/TR/2023/lr5a4.html

to provide income — but our lifespans can be unpredictably long, perhaps longer than our resources allow. Also, longer lives don't necessarily equate with healthier lives. The longer you live, the more money you will likely need to spend on health care, even excluding long-term care needs like nursing homes.

You will also run into inflation. If you don't plan to live another twenty-five years but end up doing so, inflation at an average of 3 percent will approximately double the price of goods over that time period.

Because we don't necessarily get to have our cake and eat it, too, our collective increased longevity hasn't necessarily increased the healthy years of our lives. Typically, our life-extending care most widely applies to the time in our lives when we will need more care in general. Think of common situations like a pacemaker at eighty-five or cancer treatment at seventy-eight.

"Wow, Russ," I can hear you say. "Way to start with the good news first."

I know, I've painted a grim picture, but all I'm concerned about here is cost. It's hard to put a dollar sign on life, but that is essentially what we're talking about when discussing longevity and finances. Living longer isn't a bad thing; it just costs more, and one key to a sound retirement strategy is preparing for it in advance.

My grandma is a good example of this. My grandparents raised seven children. Grandpa drove a road grader for the county, and Grandma worked at the local grocery store. Grandpa died early in his retirement when I was in high school, but my grandma lived for a long time after that. There were many trips to the doctor, medications, and procedures to keep her going.

Despite a modest financial situation, Grandma had still managed to squirrel away some money in CDs at the bank. She had zero plans of using the money in her lifetime, but she still had them just in case. It was a good thing she had done that because in her later years, she had a little cushion to fall back on when health care got expensive.

She also had four daughters who lived locally, which also helped financially. I guess when you have seven kids you deserve to have at least one stick around, and she was blessed with multiple. While she might not have been as mobile in her final years, it was special that she got to see a few great-grandchildren be born and have more time with her kids and grandkids.

Living longer may be more expensive, but it can be so meaningful when you plan for your "just-in-cases."

## Retiring Early

A key part of planning for retirement revolves around retirement income. After all, retirement is cutting the cord that tethers you to your employer — and your monthly check. However, that check often comes with many other benefits, particularly health care. Health care is often the thing that can unexpectedly put dreams for an early retirement on hold. Some employers offer health benefits to their retired workers, but that number has declined drastically over the past several decades.

In 1988, among employers who offered health benefits to their workers, 66 percent offered health benefits to their retirees. That number dwindled to 21 percent in 2023.[4] So, with employer-offered retirement health benefits on the wane, this becomes a major point of concern for anyone who is looking to retire, particularly those who are looking to retire before age sixty-five, when they would become eligible for Medicare coverage.

Fidelity estimates that the average retired couple at age sixty-five will need approximately $315,000 for health care

4 Tricia Neuman. Anthony Damico. Henry J. Kaiser Family Foundation. April 12, 2024. "Retiree Health Benefits: Going, Going, Nearly Gone?" https://www.kff.org/medicare/issue-brief/retiree-health-benefits-going-going-nearly-gone/

expenses in retirement, not including long-term care.[5] Do you think it's likely that cost will decrease?

Even if you are working until age sixty-five or have plans to cover your health expenses until that point, I often have clients who incorrectly assume Medicare is their golden ticket to cover all expenses. That is simply not the case.

## Retiring Later

Planning for a long life in retirement partly depends on when you retire. While many people end up retiring earlier than they anticipated — due to injuries, layoffs, family crises, and other unforeseen circumstances — continuing to work past age sixty (and even sixty-five) is still a viable option for others and can be an excellent way to help establish financial confidence in retirement.

There are many reasons for this. For one, you obviously still earn a paycheck and the benefits accompanying it. Medical coverage and beefing up your retirement accounts with further savings can be significant by themselves, but continuing to generate income should also keep you from dipping into your retirement funds, further allowing them the opportunity to grow.

Additionally, for many workers, their nine-to-five job is more than just clocking in and out. Having a sense of purpose can keep us active physically, mentally, and socially. That kind of activity and level of engagement may also help stave off many of the health problems that plague retirees. Avoiding a sedentary life is one of the advantages of staying plugged into the workforce, if possible.

I have a client named Jim who continued to work, not because he had to, but because he wanted to. He came to us to

---

[5] Fidelity. June 20, 2024. "Keys to covering health care in retirement" https://www.fidelity.com/learning-center/wealth-management-insights/how-to-prepare-for-health-care-costs-in-retirement

find out if it was possible for him to retire, and if so, what would that would look like.

We told him that thanks to the hard work and savings he'd put in over the years, he could do things on his terms. He ended up working another five years after that, and I distinctly remember him telling me that it no longer felt like he was going to work.

He chose to keep going because he wanted to leave his legacy at work. He explained that he was the only one at work who knew how to do a certain function, and he felt obligated to stay on until a capable replacement was found and he could teach him or her everything he knew. I found that to be fascinating because he worked for General Motors. I thought, of the hundreds of thousands of people that work there, for Jim to be the only one that had that knowledge was impressive! That was Jim's version of leaving a legacy.

## Health Care

Take a second to reflect on your health care plan. Although working up to or even past age sixty-five could allow you to avoid a coverage gap between your working years and Medicare, that may not be an option for you. Even if it is, when you retire, you will need to make some decisions about what kind of insurance coverage you may need to supplement your Medicare. Are there any medical needs you have that may require coverage in addition to Medicare? Did your parents or grandparents have any inherited medical conditions you might consider using a special savings plan to cover?

These are all questions that are important to review with your financial professional so you can be sure you have enough money put aside for health care.

# Long-Term Care

Longevity means the need for long-term care is statistically more likely to happen. If you intend to pass on a legacy, planning for long-term care is paramount since most estimates project nearly 70 percent of Americans who reach age sixty-five will need some type of it.[6] However, this may be one of the biggest, most stressful pieces of longevity planning I encounter in my work. For one thing, who wants to talk about the point in their lives when they may feel the most limited? Who wants to dwell on what will happen if they can no longer toilet, bathe, dress, or feed themselves?

I get it; this is a less-than-fun part of planning. But a little bit of preparation now can go a long way!

When it comes to your longevity, just like with your goals, one of the important things to do is sit and dream. It may not be the fun, road-trip-to-the-Grand-Canyon kind of dreaming, but you can spend time envisioning how you want your twilight years to look.

For instance, if it is important for you to live in your home for as long as possible, who will provide for the day-to-day fixes and to-dos of housework if you become ill? Will you set aside money for a service, or do you have relatives or friends nearby whom you could comfortably allow to help you? Do you prefer in-home care over a nursing home or assisted living? This could be a good time to discuss the possibility of moving into a retirement community versus staying where you are or whether it's worth moving to another state and leaving relatives behind.

These are all important factors to discuss with your spouse and children, as *now* is the right time to address questions and concerns. For instance, is aging in place more important to one spouse than the other? Are the friends or relatives who live

---

[6] Claire Samuels. A Place for Mom. September 13, 2023. "Long-Term Care Statistics: A Portrait of Americans in Assisted Living, Nursing Homes, and Skilled Nursing Facilities" https://www.aplaceformom.com/senior-living-data/articles/long-term-care-statistics

nearby emotionally, physically, and financially capable of helping you for a time if you face an illness?

Many families I meet with find these conversations very uncomfortable, particularly when children discuss nursing home care with their parents. A knee-jerk reaction for many is to promise they will care for their aging parents. This is noble and well-intentioned, but there needs to be an element of realism here. Does "help" from an adult child mean they stop by and help you with laundry, cooking, home maintenance, and bills? Or does it mean they move you into their spare room when you have hip surgery? Are they prepared to help you use the restroom and bathe if that becomes difficult for you to do on your own?

I don't mean to discourage families from caring for their own; this can be a profoundly admirable relationship when it works out. However, I've seen families put off planning for late-in-life care based on a tenuous promise that the adult children would care for their parents, only to watch as the support system crumbles. Sometimes, this is because the assumed caregiver hasn't given serious thought to the preparation they would need, both in a formal sense and regarding their personal physical, emotional, and financial commitments. This is often also because we can't see the future: Alzheimer's disease and other maladies of old age can exact a heavy toll. When a loved one reaches the point where they are at risk of wandering away or need help with two or more activities of daily living, it can be more than one person or a family can realistically handle.

If you know what you want, communicate with your family about both the best-case and worst-case scenarios. Then, hope for the best and plan for the worst.

## Realistic Cost of Care

Included in your planning should be a consideration for the cost of long-term care. The potential costs for such care and treatment can be underestimated, especially by those who have maintained robust health and find it difficult to envision future declines in their condition.

Another piece of planning for long-term care costs is anticipating inflation. It's common knowledge that prices have been and keep rising, which can lower your purchasing power on everything from food to medical care. Long-term care is a big piece of the inflation-disparity pie.

While local costs vary from state to state, the following table shows the national averages for various forms of long-term care (plus projections that account for a 3 percent annual inflation, so you can see what I am referencing):[7]

| Long-Term Care Costs: Inflation | | | | |
|---|---|---|---|---|
| | Informal Care | Home Care | Assisted Living | Nursing Home (semi-private room) |
| Annual 2024 | $42,037 | $38,591 | $65,131 | $105,921 |
| Annual 2034 | $56,495 | $51,864 | $87,531 | $149,412 |
| Annual 2044 | $78,202 | $71,791 | $121,163 | $218,137 |
| Annual 2054 | $102,036 | $93,672 | $158,090 | $297,298 |

## Fund Your Long-Term Care

One common mistake I see occurs in those who haven't planned for long-term care because they assume the government will provide everything. But that's a big misconception. The

[7] Nationwide. 2024. "Compare long-term Care costs from state to state" https://nationwidefinancialltcmap.hvsfinancial.com/

government has two health insurance programs: Medicare and Medicaid. These can greatly assist you in your health care *needs* in retirement but usually don't provide enough coverage to cover all your health care *costs* in retirement. My firm isn't a government outpost, so we don't get to make decisions regarding policy and specifics about either of these programs. I'm going to give an overview of both, but if you want to dive into the details of these programs, you can visit www.Medicare.gov and www.Medicaid.gov.

### *Medicare*

Medicare covers those aged sixty-five and older and those who are disabled. Medicare's coverage of any nursing-home-related health issues is limited. It might cover your nursing home stay if it is not a "custodial" stay and isn't long-term. For example, if you break a bone or suffer a stroke, stay in a nursing home for rehabilitative care, and then return home, Medicare may cover you. However, if you have developed dementia or are looking to move to a nursing facility because you can no longer bathe, dress, toilet, feed yourself, or take care of your hygiene, etc., then Medicare is not going to pay for your nursing home costs.[8]

You can enroll in Medicare anytime during the three months before and three months after your sixty-fifth birthday. Miss your enrollment deadline, and you could risk paying increased premiums for the rest of your life.[9] On top of prompt enrollment, there are a few other things to think about when it comes to Medicare, not least among them being the need to understand the different "parts," what they do, and what they don't cover.

---

[8] Medicare. 2024. "What Part A covers" https://www.medicare.gov/providers-services/original-medicare/part-a

[9] Medicare. 2024. "When can I sign up for Medicare?" https://www.medicare.gov/basics/get-started-with-medicare/sign-up/when-can-i-sign-up-for-medicare

## Part A

Medicare Part A is what you might think of as "classic" Medicare. Hospital care, some types of home health care, and major medical care fall under this. While most enrollees pay nothing for this service (as they likely paid into the system for at least ten years), you might have to, based on either work history or delayed signup. In 2024, the highest premium is $505 per month, and a hospital stay does have a deductible – $1,632.[10] Also, if you have a hospital stay that surpasses sixty days, you could be looking at additional costs; keep in mind, Medicare doesn't pay for long-term care and services.

## Part B

Medicare Part B is an essential piece of wrap-around coverage for Medicare Part A. It helps pay for doctor visits and outpatient services. This also comes with a price tag: Although the Part B annual deductible is only $240 in 2024, you will still pay 20 percent of all costs after that, with no limit on out-of-pocket expenses. The Part B monthly premium for 2024 ranges from the standard amount of $174.70 to $594.[11]

## Part C

Medicare Part C (more commonly known as a Medicare Advantage plan) is an alternative to a combination of Parts A, B, and sometimes D. Administered through private insurance companies, these have a variety of costs and restrictions, and they are subject to the specific policies and rules of the issuing carrier.

---

[10] Centers for Medicare & Medicaid Services. October 11, 2023. "2024 Medicare Parts A & B Premiums and Deductibles" https://www.cms.gov/newsroom/fact-sheets/2024-medicare-parts-b-premiums-and-deductibles?ref=biztoc.com

[11] Ibid.

## Part D

Medicare Part D is also offered through a private insurer and is supplemental to Parts A and B, as its primary purpose is to cover prescription drugs. Like any private insurance plan, Part D has its quirks and rules that vary from insurer to insurer.

### *The Donut Hole*

Even with a "Part D" in place, you may still have a coverage gap between what your Part D private drug insurance pays for your prescription and what basic Medicare pays. In 2024, the coverage gap is $5,030, meaning that after you meet your private prescription insurance limit, you will spend no more than 25 percent of your drug costs out-of-pocket before Medicare kicks in to pay for more prescription drugs.[12]

Note: In the donut hole, you pay up to 25 percent out of pocket for all covered medications. You leave the donut hole once you've spent $8,000 out of pocket for covered drugs in 2024. 2024 is the last year for the donut hole. A $2,000 out-of-pocket cap takes effect for Medicare Part D in 2025.

## Medicare Supplements

Medicare Supplement Insurance, MedSupp, Medigap, or offerings labeled Medicare Plan F, G, H, I, J ... Known by a variety of monikers, this is just a fancy way of saying "medical coverage for those over sixty-five that picks up the tab for whatever the federal Medicare program(s) doesn't." Again, costs, limitations, etc., vary by carrier.

Does that sound like a bunch of government alphabet soup to you? It certainly does to me. And did you read the fine print? Unpredictable costs, varied restrictions, difficult-to-compare benefits, donut holes, and coverage gaps. That's par for the

---

[12] Medicare. 2024. "Costs in the coverage gap" https://www.medicare.gov/drug-coverage-part-d/costs-for-medicare-drug-coverage/costs-in-the-coverage-gap

course with health care plans throughout our adult lives. What gives? I thought Medicare was supposed to be easier, comprehensive, and at no cost!

The truth is there is probably no stage of life when health care is easy to understand.

Television commercials with famous people like William Shatner, George Foreman, and Joe Namath are meant to build trust with the viewer. However, there is no number of celebrity appearances that will make things easier to navigate. So when it comes to something as specialized as Medicare, we bring in someone whose primary focus is to understanding and being skillful at guiding people to make the right decision for their particular situation.

One of the best things you can do for yourself is to scope out the health care field early, compare costs often, and prepare for out-of-pocket costs well in advance — decades, if possible.

### *Medicaid*

Medicaid is a program the states administer, so funding, protocol, and limitations vary. Compared to Medicare, Medicaid more widely covers nursing home care but targets a different demographic: those with low incomes.

If you have more assets than the Medicaid limit in your state and need nursing home care, you will need to use those assets to pay for your care. You will also have a list of additional state-approved ways to use or spend some of these assets over the Medicaid limit, such as pre-purchasing burial plots and funeral expenses or paying off debts. After that, your remaining assets fund your nursing home stay until they are gone, at which point Medicaid will jump in.

Some people aren't stymied by this, thinking they will just pass on their financial assets early by gifting them to relatives, friends, and causes so they can qualify for Medicaid when they need it. However, to prevent this exact scenario, Uncle Sam has implemented what's called the "look-back period." Currently, if you enroll in Medicaid, you are subject to having the government scrutinize the last five years of your finances for large gifts or expenses that may subject you to penalties, temporarily making you ineligible for Medicaid coverage.

So, if you're planning to preserve your money for future generations and retain control of your financial resources during your lifetime, you'll probably want to prepare for the costs of longevity beyond a "government plan."

### *Self-Funding*

One way to fund a longer life is the old-fashioned way, through self-funding. There are a variety of financial tools you can use, and they all have their pros and cons. If your assets are in low-interest financial vehicles (savings, bonds, CDs), you risk letting inflation erode the value of your dollar. If you are relying on the stock market, you have more growth potential, but you'll also want to consider the possible implications of market volatility. What if your assets take a hit? If you suffer a loss in your retirement portfolio in early or mid-retirement, you might have the option to "tighten your belt," so to speak, and cut back on discretionary spending to allow your portfolio the room to bounce back. But if you are retired and depend on income from a stock account that just hit a downward stride, what are you going to do?

### *HSAs*

These days, you might also be able to self-fund through a health savings account (HSA) if you have access to one through a high-deductible health plan (you will not qualify to save in an HSA after enrolling in Medicare). In an HSA, any growth of your tax-deductible contributions will be tax-free, and any distributions paid out for qualified health costs are also tax-free. Long-term care expenses count as health costs, so if this option is available to you, it is one way to use the tax advantages to self-fund your longevity. Bear in mind if you are younger than sixty-five, any money you use for non-qualified expenses will be subject to taxes and penalties, and if you are older than sixty-five, any

HSA money you use for non-medical expenses is subject to income tax.

### *LTCI*

One slightly more nuanced way to pay for longevity — specifically for long-term care — is long-term care insurance (LTCI). As car insurance protects your assets in case of a car accident and home insurance protects your assets in case something happens to your house, long-term care insurance aims to protect your assets in case you need long-term care in an at-home or nursing home situation.

As with other types of insurance, you will pay a monthly or annual premium in exchange for an insurance company paying for long-term care down the road. Typically, policies cover two to three years of care, which is adequate for an "average" situation: it's estimated that 70 percent of Americans aged sixty-five and older will need long-term care of some kind.[13]

Now, there are a few oft-cited components of LTCI that make it unattractive for some:

- Expense — LTCI can be expensive. It is generally less expensive the younger you are, but a sixty-five-year-old man would pay about $2,749 annually, while a woman that age would pay about $4,599 annually for a similar policy.[14] The annual cost typically increases from there, as you age.
- Limited options — LTCI may be expensive for consumers, but it can also be expensive for companies that offer it. With fewer companies willing to take on that expense, the market narrows, limiting

[13] Claire Samuels. A Place for Mom. September 13, 2023. "Long-Term Care Statistics: A Portrait of Americans in Assisted Living, Nursing Homes, and Skilled Nursing Facilities" https://www.aplaceformom.com/senior-living-data/articles/long-term-care-statistics

[14] Joshua Rodriguez. CBS News. May 1, 2024. "How much does long-term care insurance cost for a 65-year-old?" https://www.cbsnews.com/news/how-much-does-long-term-care-insurance-cost-for-a-65-year-old/

opportunities to price shop for policies with different options or custom benefits.

- If you know you need it, you might not be able to get it — Insurance companies offering LTCI are taking on a risk that you may need LTCI. That risk is the foundation of the product — you may or may not need it. If you know you will need it because you have a dementia diagnosis or another illness for which you will need long-term care, you will likely not qualify for LTCI coverage.
- Use it or lose it — If you have LTCI and are in the minority of Americans who die having never needed long-term care, all the money you paid into your LTCI policy is gone.
- Possibly fluctuating rates — Your premium rate is not locked in on LTCI. Companies maintain the ability to raise or lower your premium amounts. This means some seniors face an ultimatum: Keep funding a policy at what might be a less affordable rate *or* lose coverage and let go of all the money they have paid so far.

After that, you might be thinking, "How can people possibly be interested in LTCI?" But let me repeat myself — it's anticipated that as many as 70 percent of Americans will need long-term care. And although only one in ten Americans aged fifty-five-plus has purchased LTCI, keep in mind the high cost of nursing home care. Can you afford $7,000 a month to put into nursing home care and still have enough left over to help protect your legacy? This is a genuine concern, not only because of the statistics about long-term care needs mentioned above but also because nearly a third of American seniors will die with some level of cognitive impairment — including the roughly 10 percent who currently have Alzheimer's.[15] So, not to sound like a broken record, but it is vitally important to have a plan in

[15] Alzheimer's Association. 2024. "Alzheimer's Disease Facts and Figures" https://www.alz.org/alzheimers-dementia/facts-figures

place to deal with longevity and long-term care, especially if you intend to leave a financial legacy.

A few relevant statistics to keep in mind:

- The longer you live, the more health care you will likely need to pay for.
- The median cost of a private nursing home room in the United States between 2022 and 2023 was $10.025 a month.[16] But keep in mind that is just the nursing home — it doesn't include other medical costs, let alone pleasantries like entertainment or hobby spending.
- As referenced earlier, Fidelity calculated in a 2022 study that a healthy couple retiring at age sixty-five could expect to pay around $315,000 over the course of retirement to cover health and medical expenses.

I know. "Whoa, there, Russ, I was hoping to have a realistic idea of health costs, not be driven over by a cement mixer!"

The good news is, while we don't know these exact costs in advance, we know there *will* be costs. And you won't have to pay your total Medicare lifetime premiums in one day as a lump sum. Now that you have a good idea of health care costs in retirement, you can *plan* for them! That's the real point here: Planning in advance can keep you from feeling nickel-and-dimed to your wits' end. Instead, having a sizeable portion of your assets earmarked for health care can allow you the freedom to choose health care networks, coverage options, and long-term care possibilities that you like.

### ***Product Riders***

LTCI and self-funding are not the only ways to plan for the expenses of longevity. Some companies are getting creative with their products, particularly insurance companies. One way they are retooling to meet people's needs is through optional product riders on annuities and life insurance. Elsewhere in

---

[16] Jeff Hoyt. Senior Living. October 3, 2024. "Nursing Home Costs in 2024" https://www.seniorliving.org/nursing-homes/costs/

this book, I talk about annuity basics, but here's a brief overview: Annuities are insurance contracts. You pay the insurance company a premium — either as a lump sum or as a series of payments over a set amount of time — in exchange for guaranteed income payments.

One of the advantages of an annuity is it has access to riders, which allow you to tweak your contract for a fee, depending on the type and length of the coverage. On average, FIA fees cost up to 1.25 percent annually.[17] One annuity rider some companies offer is a long-term care rider. If you have an annuity with a long-term care rider and do not require long-term care, your contract behaves as any annuity contract would — nothing changes. Generally speaking, if you reach a point when you can't perform multiple functions of daily life on your own, you notify the insurance company, and if you meet the long-term care rider requirements, your additional rider benefits can be activated to help you pay for your long-term care needs. An insurance company representative will turn on those provisions of your contract. Activating LTC rider benefits is more involved than simply calling your insurance carrier. A physician has to confirm that you cannot perform the required amount of activities of daily living (ADLs).

Like LTCI, different companies and products offer different options. Some annuity long-term care riders offer coverage of two years in a nursing home situation. Others cap expenses at two times the original annuity's value. It greatly depends. Some people prefer this option because there isn't a "use-it-or-lose-it" piece; if you die without ever having needed long-term care, you still will have had the income benefit from the base contract.

Still, as with any annuities or insurance contracts, there are the usual restrictions and limitations. Withdrawing money from the contract will affect future income payments, early distributions can result in a penalty, income taxes may apply,

[17] Shawn Plummer. The Annuity Expert. 2024. "A Guide To Annuity Fees" https://www.annuityexpertadvice.com/types-of-annuities/annuity-fees/

and because the insurance company's solvency is what guarantees your payments, it's important to do your research about the insurance company you are considering purchasing a contract from.

Understandably, a discussion on long-term care is bound to feel at least a little tedious. Yet, this is an important piece of planning for income in retirement, particularly if you want to leave a legacy.

There is a specific lens we look through when determining what approach you should take toward addressing long-term care expenses. I believe most people fall into one of three categories:

The first is that they are in a shortage position for retirement. This means that they aren't on track to have enough to live on. For those folks, their money should probably go towards saving for retirement, as insurance is more of a luxury item. And if they do need long-term care, then Medicaid could be the solution for them.

The other end of the spectrum would be the second category, and that is the people that are in a surplus retirement situation. Not just a slight surplus, either. This is one that when we model their retirement plan and plug in a hypothetical long-term care expense over multiple years, it still shows a surplus. This would be where self-insuring could be the appropriate path. This means they would pay the cost out-of-pocket when that time comes and not pay premiums to an insurance company.

Then there is the third category. This is the group of people who will probably have a comfortable retirement and are on track or who aren't that far off. For these people, life is good unless that large medical expense comes into play. This would be where we want to look at options to transfer that large risk that you cannot afford over to an insurance company.

# Spousal Planning

Here's one thing to keep in mind no matter how you plan to save: Many of us will be planning for more than ourselves. Look back at all the stats on health events and the likelihood of long life and long-term care. If they hold true for a single individual, then the likelihood of having a costly health or long-term care event is even higher for a married couple. You'll be planning for not just one life but two. So, when it comes to long-term care insurance, annuities, self-funding, or whatever strategy you are considering, be sure you are funding longevity for the both of you.

CHAPTER 2

# Taxes

Where to begin with taxes? Perhaps by acknowledging we all bear responsibility for the resources we share, such as roads, bridges, and schools. Every American's patriotic duty is to pay their fair share of taxes. Many would agree with me. However, while they don't mind paying their fair share, they're not interested in paying one cent more than that!

Now, just talking about taxes probably takes your mind to April — tax season. You are probably thinking about all the forms you collect and how you file. Perhaps you are thinking about your certified public accountant or another qualified tax professional and saying to yourself, "I've already got taxes taken care of — thanks!"

However, what I see when people come into my office is that their relationship with their tax professional is purely a January through April relationship. That means they may have a tax *professional* but not a tax *planner*.

What I mean is tax planning extends beyond filing taxes. In April, we are required to settle our accounts with the IRS to make sure we have paid up on our bill or even the score if we have overpaid. Yet real tax planning is about making each financial move in a way that allows you to keep the most money in your pocket and out of Uncle Sam's.

Now, as a caveat, I want to emphasize I am neither a CPA nor a tax planner, but I see the way taxes affect my clients, and I have plenty of experience helping clients implement tax-efficient strategies in their retirement plans in conjunction with their tax professionals.

It is especially important to me to help my clients develop tax-efficient strategies in their retirement plans because each dollar they can keep in their pockets is a dollar we can put to work.

Many people I've talked to from past generations believed you should kick the tax can down the road. We hear that we should be saving into our pretax 401(k)/403(b)/457/IRA while we are in our peak earning years so that we can pull it out in retirement and pay a lower tax rate then.

I ask you to strongly consider this question, though: Will you actually be in a lower tax bracket in retirement? Maybe. Maybe not. Everyone's situation is truly unique, and we don't know for sure, so be careful of blanket statements. What I can tell you is this: I have had conversations with thousands of people in my career about retirement, and I have not met anyone, not one single person, who told me they would like to reduce their lifestyle in retirement.

If lifestyles are staying the same or increasing due to more travel, then what is needed? You'll need just as much or more income in retirement. If you are like most Americans who have most of their money in a pretax place, when you go to turn that on for income, it will be taxable. Yes, I know, you might not be commuting to work anymore or don't need expensive work clothes, and so expenses like these will go away. However, these expenses could very well be replaced with extra trips or experiences or spoiling the grandkids.

## The Fed

Now, in the United States, taxes can be a rather uncertain proposition. Depending on who is in the White House and which party controls Congress, we might be tempted to assume tax rates could either decline or increase in the next four to eight years accordingly. However, there is one (large!) factor we, as a nation, must confront: the national debt.

Currently, according to USDebtClock.org, we are over $35,000,000,000,000 in debt and climbing. That's $35 *trillion* with a "T." With just $1 trillion, you could park it in the bank at a zero percent interest rate and spend more than $54 million every day for fifty years without hitting a zero balance.

Even if Congress got a handle on that debt and stopped its daily compound, divided by each taxpayer, we each would owe about $271,000. So, will that be check, cash, or Venmo?[18]

My point here isn't to give you anxiety. I'm just cautioning you that even with the rosiest of outlooks on our personal income tax rates, none of us should count on low tax rates for the long term. Instead, you and your network of professionals (tax, legal, and financial) should constantly be looking for ways to take advantage of tax-saving opportunities as they come.

So, how can we get started?

## Know Your Limits

One of the foundational pieces of tax planning is knowing and understanding your marginal tax rate. Marginal tax rate is the tax rate you pay on your highest dollar of income. In the United States, we use a progressive tax system, meaning your marginal tax rate increases as your taxable income increases. However, to be clear, not all of your income is taxed at that highest rate — only the upper portion.

A taxpayer's income is divided into tax brackets, and the brackets determine the rate applied to increments of the filer's taxable income.

For example, if your single friend tells you she is in the 22 percent tax bracket, that means her highest amount of income is taxed at 22 percent, but chunks of her income are taxed at lower rates. Using the 2024 tax bracket below, her first $11,600

---

[18] usdebtclock.org. Accessed on October 23, 2024.

of income will be taxed at 10 percent, but her next chunk of income ($11,601 to $47,150) will be taxed at 12 percent. Finally, her income, beginning at $47,151, will be taxed at 22 percent. Her tax owed for the year — before any additional taxes or credits — is the accumulation of those three amounts.

| 2024 Tax Brackets: Single Filers | | |
|---|---|---|
| **Tax Rate** | **Taxable Income Bracket** | **Tax Owed** |
| 10% | $0 to $11,600 | 10% of taxable income. |
| 12% | $11,601 to $47,150 | $1,160 plus 12% of the amount over $11,600 |
| 22% | $47,151 to $100,525 | $5,426 plus 22% of the amount over $47,150 |
| 24% | $100,526 to $191,950 | $17,168.50 plus 24% of the amount over $100,525 |
| 32% | $191,951 to $243,725 | $39,110.50 plus 32% of the amount over $191,950 |
| 35% | $243,726 to $609,350 | $55,678.50 plus 35% of the amount over $243,725 |
| 37% | $609,351 or more | $183,647.25 plus 37% of the amount over $609,350 |

[19]

It's important to note the difference between marginal and effective tax rates. The effective tax rate represents the percentage of taxable income an individual pays in taxes. To

[19] Sabrina Parys. Tina Orem. NerdWallet. May 30, 2024. “2024 Tax Brackets and Federal Income Tax Rates” https://www.nerdwallet.com/article/taxes/federal-income-tax-brackets

calculate the effective rate, divide the total dollar amount you pay in income tax by your total income. Thus, it is the average rate and is almost always a lower percentage than a marginal rate.

Why are marginal and effective rates important in retirement planning? Federal income tax is one of the biggest expenses individuals pay in their lives. In some cases, the lifetime amount can exceed lifetime mortgage payments. Although there are federal tax breaks for Americans over the age of sixty-five, many former high-income earners continue to pay income taxes. Estimating your marginal tax rate is one of the components in determining when to begin Social Security and a crucial factor regarding Roth IRA conversions. Also, a thorough analysis of current and future marginal tax rates is important in the strategic planning for required minimum distributions (RMDs) on tax-deferred retirement accounts.

## Assuming a Lower Tax Rate

Retirement has always been imagined as a time when you stop working and no longer earn wages or self-employment income. In the past, Social Security benefits were not subject to taxation. Even though pensions were usually taxable, their income stream didn't fully replace a recipient's previous salary. If you needed to pull from your investment funds during retirement, keep in mind that the principal had already been taxed. In general, prior to the 1970s, your income during retirement – your cash inflow – was usually taxed at a lower rate than when you were working because you had less income and certain portions of it were not taxable.

In 1978, lawmakers created Section 401 of the Internal Revenue Code to prevent companies from using tax-advantaged profit-sharing plans to primarily benefit executives. However, businessman Ted Benna reimagined this code as the foundation of the modern 401(k). This innovation ultimately led to the decline of traditional company pension plans while shifting both control and risk to employees. The most significant change was the shift of taxation from when employees were paid and when investment income was earned to the time of withdrawal. This tax advantage encouraged individuals to save more money in tax-deferred plans than they would have in regular savings accounts, up to the allowed limits.

In addition, in 1983, Social Security introduced new tax brackets to address the problem of decreasing reserves. This resulted in both the potential for Social Security to become taxable and a significant shift in retirement planning strategy. Within a five-year period, the retirement planning landscape changed for decades going forward, possibly forever.

A big selling point for qualified retirement accounts (401(k)s, 403(b)s, IRAs, etc.) is the theory that people will pay less in tax during their retirement years than during their working years when they're putting that money away. The idea is that you're allowed to "defer" paying the tax on that income until your marginal tax rate drops in retirement. Hence, you pay less in tax on that income.

But what if it doesn't pan out that way? For some retirees, their marginal tax rate will stay the same in retirement or even increase. If you have a healthy balance in your qualified retirement account, combining its RMDs or even a Roth conversion with Social Security can result in what is called the "tax torpedo." This tax increase occurs when a larger percent of your Social Security becomes taxable, and that same income increase consequently bumps a taxpayer up to a higher marginal rate.

## 401(k)s/IRAs/Roth IRAs

One sometimes-unexpected piece of tax planning in retirement concerns the 401(k) or IRA. Most of us have one of these accounts or an equivalent. We pay in throughout our working lives, dutifully socking away a portion of our earnings in these tax-deferred accounts. There's the rub: tax-*deferred*, not tax-

*free*. Very rarely is anything free of taxation when you get down to it. Using 401(k)s and IRAs in retirement is no different. The taxes the government deferred when you were in your working years are now coming due, and you will pay taxes on that income at whatever your current tax rate is.

Just to ensure Uncle Sam gets his due, the government also has an RMD rule. Beginning at age seventy-three (or seventy-five if you were born in 1960 or after), you are required to withdraw a certain minimum amount every year from your 401(k) or IRA, or else you will face a tax penalty on any RMD monies you should have withdrawn but didn't — and that's on top of income tax. The SECURE Act 2.0 reduced the penalty to 25 percent (from 50 percent). Timely corrections can further reduce the penalty to 10 percent.[20]

Of course, there is also the Roth account. You can think of the difference between a Roth and a traditional retirement account as the difference between taxing the seed and taxing the harvest. Because Roths get funded with post-tax dollars, there aren't tax penalties for early withdrawals of the principal, nor are there taxes on the growth after you reach age fifty-nine-and-one-half. Perhaps best of all, there are no RMDs. Of course, you must own a Roth account for a minimum of five years before you are able to take advantage of all its features.

This is one more area where it pays to be aware of your marginal tax rate. Some people may opt to put any excess RMDs from their traditional retirement accounts into stocks or insurance. Others may find it advantageous to "convert" their traditional retirement account funds to Roth account funds in a year during which they are in a lower tax bracket.

---

[20] Jim Probasco. Investopedia. October 20, 2023. "SECURE 2.0 Act of 2022: Overview, Rules, Limits" https://www.investopedia.com/secure-2-0-definition-5225115

# Roth IRA Conversions

A Roth conversion simply means converting (or withdrawing) monies from your traditional, tax-deferred retirement accounts and moving them to a Roth account. Once inside the Roth, any growth on these funds will accumulate completely tax-free, and tax will not be owed when the Roth funds are withdrawn, assuming the conditions noted above. This is an exciting opportunity for accumulation! However, a thoughtful strategy is beneficial in the conversion process. Since dollars were placed into the traditional account pre-tax and the growth is taxable in these accounts, tax is owed on *all* the money converted to the Roth. Converting an employer plan account to a Roth IRA is a taxable event. Increased taxable income from the Roth IRA conversion may have several consequences, including (but not limited to) a need for additional tax withholding or estimated tax payments, the loss of certain tax deductions and credits, higher taxes on Social Security benefits, and higher Medicare premiums.

Points to consider regarding a conversion:

**How are you going to pay the tax?** Again, any time you withdraw funds from a 401(k) or traditional IRA, tax is owed on 100 percent of that money, whether the distribution was a basic withdrawal, an RMD, or a Roth conversion. In addition to the income tax, if the account owner is younger than fifty-nine-and-one-half, it is most likely a 10 percent tax penalty will be assessed. So, if you're under fifty-nine-and-one-half and have a year when your income is lower – reducing your marginal tax rate – you need to weigh the amount of the tax penalty against the decrease in ordinary income tax.

As a tricky sidenote, if you are under fifty-nine-and-one-half and you have tax withheld from your conversion and sent directly to the government, you will not escape the 10 percent penalty.

**Did you compare your current tax rate to your estimated future rate?** As mentioned above, a good time to consider a Roth is in a year when your taxable income — and thus your marginal tax rate — is lower than normal or lower than expected in the future. A popular conversion strategy is to transfer funds during a period referred to as "the trough years." That is the period after you've retired but before you begin receiving Social Security or are required to begin RMDs. It is easier to manage the tax on the conversion during these years as you have more control over the sources and the amounts of your income.

**What is your Roth withdrawal strategy?** There are four considerations here.

- Can you leave converted money in the Roth for at least five years? You must leave your converted money in the Roth for at least five years for the withdrawals to be tax-free. That five-year countdown begins on January 1 of the year you made the conversion, even if your conversion date was December 31. This five-year countdown applies in each year you make a conversion.
- Even if you hold the Roth funds for five years, you can still face penalties for withdrawals if you're under fifty-nine-and-one-half. The two exceptions to being penalized are using the withdrawal (up to a $ 10,000 lifetime maximum) to pay for a first-time home purchase or if you become disabled or pass away.[21]
- The longer you leave funds inside the Roth after the conversion, the more time it can grow and potentially recoup the tax levied on your traditional account's withdrawals. Remember, this money is now growing tax-free. A long growth period may be able to outweigh a loss in your balance due to income tax withholdings at conversion time. Also, an error in estimates of future tax rate margins (i.e., your future rates turned out to be less than the conversion year)

---

[21] Charles Schwab. 2024. "Roth IRA withdrawal rules" https://www.schwab.com/ira/roth-ira/withdrawal-rules

can be made up by holding funds in your Roth for many years.[22]

- Planning to use your Roth as a legacy planning tool? There are various rules and options depending on the type of heir, but in most cases the Roth is given additional time to grow tax-free.

Does that make your head spin? Understandable. That's why it's so important to work with a financial professional and tax planner who can help you execute these sorts of tax-efficient strategies and help you understand what you are doing and why.

I believe it is important to diversify your assets from a tax perspective so that you have the flexibility and can help you position yourself if taxes rise in the future. Having after-tax or tax-free assets to balance out your taxable accounts is important. This is where things like Roth IRAs and cash value inside of properly structured life insurance policies may come into play. You don't want to be forced to pay tax on every dollar you pull out of your portfolio in retirement.

Flexibility can help give you the opportunity to impact what tax bracket you end up in each year. It could potentially reduce the amount of your Social Security that is taxable. It gets me going whenever I think about the government taking tax out of my paycheck for Social Security and potentially taxing me on my Social Security income.

---

[22] Tim Steffen. Baird Private Wealth Management. October 16, 2023. "The Three Tests Before a Roth Conversion" https://www.bairdwealth.com/insights/wealth-management-perspectives/2023/09/the-three-tests-before-a-roth-conversion/

CHAPTER 3

# Market Volatility

Up and down. Roller coaster. Merry-go-round. Bulls and bears. Peak-to-trough.

Sound familiar? This is the language we use to talk about the stock market. With volatility and spikes, even our language is jarring, bracing, and vivid.

Still, financial strategies tend to revolve around market-based products, and for good reasons. For one thing, there is no other financial class that packs the same potential for growth, pound for pound, as stock-based products. Because of growth potential, inflation challenges, and new opportunities, it may be unwise to avoid the market entirely.

However, along with the potential for growth is the potential for loss. At the time this book was written, many of the people I've seen in my office came in feeling uneasy. Already in this decade, they have witnessed the economic fallout of the COVID-19 outbreak of 2020, followed by an economic downturn and the inflation spike that began in 2022.

So, how do we balance these factors? How do we try to satisfy both the need for protection and the need for growth?

For one thing, it is important to recognize the value of diversity. Now, I'm not just talking about the diversity of assets among different kinds of stocks or even different kinds of stocks and bonds. That's only one kind of diversity. Stocks and bonds, though different, are both still important market-based products. Even within a diverse portfolio, most market-based products tend to rise or fall as a whole, just like an incoming tide. Therefore, a portfolio diverse in only market-sourced products won't automatically preserve your assets when the market declines.

In addition to the sort of "horizontal diversity" you have by purchasing a variety of stocks and bonds from different companies, I also suggest you think about "vertical diversity," or diversity among asset classes. This means having different product types, including securities products, bank products, and insurance products — with varying levels of growth potential, liquidity, and asset preservation — all in accordance with your unique situation, goals, and needs.

It is important to determine your comfort level with risk in your investments. This is also called risk tolerance. As humans, we are all unique and have different sets of experiences, understanding, and relationships with money. A good way to determine the amount of risk you should take in your investments is to start with a simple question: How much money do you want to lose?

You may be thinking, "Is this a trick question, Russ?" No, it isn't. If you have $500,000 for example, and one year later you have $400,000, what would you think of that? Are you okay with that? If not, then what is your number? I would encourage you to think of it in dollars and not percentages, because when you see your statements, that is what you will be looking at. My guess is that your answer of how much you are okay losing will be a lot smaller than the amount you are chancing in your current investments. That is why we want to understand how much you are okay losing and line up your investments to match proactively, and not wait until after the market goes down.

## The Color of Money

When looking at the overall diversity of your portfolio, part of the equation is knowing which products fit in what category:

what has liquidity, what has asset preservation, and what has growth potential.

Before we dive in, keep in mind these aren't absolutes. You might think of liquidity, growth, and asset preservation as primary colors. While some products will look pretty much yellow, red, or blue, others will have a mix of characteristics, making them more green, orange, or purple.

## Growth

I like to think of the growth category as red. It's powerful, it's somewhat volatile, and it's also the category where we have the greatest opportunities for growth and loss. Products in the growth category often have a good deal of liquidity but very little asset preservation. These are our market-based products and strategies, and we think of them mostly in shades of red and orange to designate their growth and liquidity. This is usually a good place to be when you're young — think fast cars and flashy leather jackets — but its allure often wanes as you move closer to retirement. Examples of "red" products include:

- Stocks
- Equities
- Exchange-traded funds
- Mutual funds
- Corporate bonds
- Real estate investment trusts
- Speculations
- Alternative investments

## Liquidity

Yellow is my liquid category color. I typically recommend having at least enough yellow money to cover six months to a year's worth of expenses in case of emergency. Yellow assets don't need a lot of growth potential; they just need to be readily available when we need them. The "yellow" category includes assets like:

- Cash
- Money market accounts

## Asset Preservation

To me, the color of asset preservation is blue, which can incorporate products such as annuities. Tranquil, sure — even if it lacks a certain amount of flash. This is the direction I like to see people generally move toward as they're nearing retirement. The red, flashy look of stock market returns and the risk of possible overnight losses are less attractive as we near retirement and look for more consistency and reliability. While this category doesn't come with a lot of liquidity, the products here are backed by an insurance company, a bank, or a government entity. "Blue" products include things such as:

- Certificates of deposit (backed by banks)
- Government-based bonds (backed by the U.S. government)
- Life insurance (backed by insurance companies)
- Annuities (backed by insurance companies)

Since you won't be spending all of your money at the same time (or if you are, it must be one hell of a party, so please invite us), we don't want to treat all of your money the same way. You want to have buckets of money that are protected and accessible for the early years.

For the middle years, you want a degree of protection which will also target a little higher potential return. And for the money you don't need for over a decade from now, we will want to allocate that for longer-term growth opportunities and let that be a possible hedge against long-term inflation and longevity risk.

As a result, the best outcomes are often more easily obtained by using a wide mix of investment types. Every investment instrument out there has something we like about it, and on the other side of the coin, there is going to be a detractor. By diversifying the types of investments, the goal is to have the features we like about something offset the features we don't like about something else.

## 401(k)s

I want to take a second to specifically address a product many retirees will use to build their retirement income: the 401(k) and other retirement accounts. Any of these retirement accounts (IRAs, 401(k)s, 403(b)s, etc.) are basically "tax wrappers." What do I mean by that? Well, depending on your plan provider, a 401(k) could include target-date funds, passively managed products, stocks, bonds, mutual funds, or even variable, fixed, and fixed index annuities, all collected in one place and governed by rules (a.k.a. the "tax wrapper"). These rules govern how much money you can put inside, how you can put it in, when you pay taxes on it, and when you can take the money out. Inside the 401(k), each of the products inside the "tax wrapper" might have its own fees or commissions in addition to the management fee you pay on the 401(k) itself.

Now, fees can be troublesome. You can't get something for nothing, and fees are how many financial companies and professionals make a living. Yet, it's important to recognize that even a fee with a fraction of a percentage point is money out of your pocket — money that represents not just the one-time fee of today but also an opportunity cost. For example, consider how a $100,000 IRA that earns 6 percent over a twenty-five-year period without investment fees would earn $430,000. But if just a 0.5 percent fee was factored into that investment, the IRA would be worth $379,000 in twenty-five years — a $50,500 decrease. For someone close to retirement, how much do you think fees may have cost over their lifetime?

Even for those close to retirement, it's important to look at management fees and assess if you think you're getting what you pay for. Over the course of ten years, those costs can add up, and you may have decades ahead of you in which you will need to rely on your assets.

## Dollar-Cost Averaging

With 401(k)s and other market-based retirement products, dollar-cost averaging is a concept that can work in your favor when you are investing for the long term. When the market is trending up, if you are consistently paying in money, month over month, great; your investments can grow, and you are adding to your assets. When the market takes a dip, no problem; your dollars buy more shares at a lower price. At some point, we hope the market will rebound, in which case your shares can grow and possibly be more valuable than they were before. This concept is what we call "dollar-cost averaging." While it can't ensure a profit or guarantee against losses, it's a time-tested strategy for investing in a volatile market.

However, when you are in retirement, this strategy may work against you. You may have heard of "reverse" dollar-cost averaging. Before, when the market lost ground, you were "bargain-shopping"; your dollars purchased more assets at a reduced price. When you are in retirement, you are no longer the purchaser; you are selling. So, in a down market, you have to sell more assets to make the same amount of money as what you made in a favorable market.

I've had lots of people step into my office to talk to me about this, emphasizing how their advisor says, "The market always bounces back, and I have to just hold on for the long term."

There's some basis for this thinking; thus far, the market has always rebounded to higher heights than before. But this is no guarantee, and the prospect of potentially higher returns in five years may not be very helpful in retirement if you are relying on the income from those returns to pay this month's electric bill, for example.

It is about time in the market, not timing the market. To be prepared for whatever the markets may bring our way, we believe it's important to take what's called a "core with satellites" approach. This might mean owning things you often can't get inside of an employer-sponsored plan. In theory, most of your growth money would be in the core. This is designed to be a low-cost, broad, long-term approach that rebalances and monitors for overlap and style drift. If you have heard of modern portfolio theory or asset allocation, this is where that would come into play.

To add an additional layer of diversification, we want to add satellite strategies. Each satellite is unique in its approach. Some might be more of a tactical strategy, meaning it will be more actively traded and quick to play defense if there is unusually high volatility. Another might be a "theme" investment, that seeks to position itself to take advantage of current events. For example, as interests are rising, historically bank and insurance company stocks have done well, so it may concentrate in those areas. Or in times of high inflation, real assets such as precious metals, oil, and real estate tend to do well. Another satellite for those who qualify and are comfortable with the risks would be owning things that are not publicly traded. Owning stocks in companies that are late-stage startups but haven't yet been listed on a public exchange can add a unique growth element and also be a piece that doesn't move up and down with the emotions of the market as it isn't listed on an exchange. Each strategy comes with its own unique goal and corresponding risks, so you'll want to work with an experienced advisor for this approach.

Just like satellites orbiting the Earth, these satellites will be rotated in and out when it makes sense to do so. The core and satellite approach provides not just diversification of asset classes, but also diversification of management styles, which over time can help reduce risk and increase the potential for returns.

## Is There a "Perfect" Product?

To bring us back around to the discussion of asset preservation, growth, and liquidity, the ideal product would be a "ten" in all three categories, right? Completely guaranteed, doubling in size every few years, and accessible whenever you want. Does such a product exist? Absolutely not.

Instead of running in circles looking for that perfect product, the silver bullet, the unicorn of financial strategies, it's more important to circle back to the concept of a balanced, asset-diverse portfolio.

This is why it could be prudent to work with a knowledgeable financial professional who knows what various financial products can do and how to use them in your personal retirement strategy.*

* Investing involves risk, including the potential loss of principal. No investment strategy can guarantee a profit or protect against loss in periods of declining values. Any references to protection benefits or guaranteed/lifetime income streams refer only to fixed insurance products, not securities or investment products. Insurance and annuity product guarantees are backed by the financial strength and claims-paying ability of the issuing insurance company.

CHAPTER 4

# Retirement Income

Retirement. For many of us, it's what we've saved for and dreamed of, pinning our hopes to a magical someday. Is that someday full of traveling? Is it filled with grandkids? Gardening? Maybe your fondest dream is simply never having to work again, never having to clock in or be accountable to someone else.

Your ability to do these things all hinges on *income*. Without the money to support these dreams, even a basic level of work-free lifestyle is unsustainable. That's why planning for your income in retirement is so foundational. But where do we begin?

It's easy to feel overwhelmed by this question. Some may feel the urge to amass a large lump sum and then try to put it all in one product — insurance, investments, liquid assets — to provide all the growth, liquidity, and income they need. Instead, I think you need a more balanced approach. After all, retirement planning isn't magic. As I mention elsewhere, no single product can be all things to all people (or even all things to one person). No approach works unilaterally for everyone. That's why it's important to talk to a financial professional who can help you lay down the basics and take you step-by-step through the process. Not only will you have the assurance you have addressed the areas you need to, but you will also have an ally who can help you break down the process and help keep you from feeling overwhelmed.

# Sources of Income

Thinking of all the pieces of your retirement expenses might be intimidating. But, like cleaning out a junk drawer or revisiting that garage remodel, once you have laid everything out, you can begin to sort things into categories.

Once you have a good overall picture of where your expenses will lie, you can start stacking up the resources to cover them.

## Social Security

Social Security is a guaranteed, inflation-adjusted federal insurance program that plays a significant part in most of our retirement plans. From delaying until you've reached full retirement age or beyond to examining spousal benefits, as I discuss elsewhere in this book, there is plenty you can do to try to make the most of this monthly benefit. As with all your retirement income sources, it's important to consider ways to stretch this resource to provide the most bang for your situation.

## Pension

Another generally reliable source of retirement income for you might be a pension if you are one of the lucky people who still has one.

If you don't have a pension, go ahead and skim on to the next section. If you do have a pension, keep on reading.

Because your pension can be such a central piece of your retirement income plan, you will want to put some thought into answering basic questions about it.

How well is your pension funded? Since the heyday of the pension plan, companies and governments have neglected to fund their pension obligations, causing a persistent problem with this otherwise reliable asset.

Consider the factors at play, though. Pensions had been underfunded and gained a boost from strong market performance, most recently in 2021.[23] What happens to the solvency of those pension funds if the market declines?

It can be worthwhile to keep tabs on your pension's health and know your options for withdrawing from it. Typically, you have one chance at electing the distribution option at your retirement with no recourse to change at a later date, so you will want to look at all options before making a final decision. If you have already retired and made those decisions, this may be a foregone conclusion. If not, it pays to know what you can expect and what decisions you can make, such as taking spousal options to cover your spouse if they outlive you.

Also, some companies are incentivizing lump-sum payouts of pensions to reduce the companies' payment liabilities. If that's the case with your employer, talk to your financial professional to see if it might be prudent to do something like that or if it might be better to stick with lifetime payments or other options.

## Your 401(k) and IRA

One "modern way" to save for retirement is in a 401(k) or IRA (or their nonprofit or governmental equivalents). These tax-advantaged accounts are, in my opinion, a poor substitute for pensions, but one of the biggest disservices we do to ourselves is not taking full advantage of them in the first place. While the average 401(k) balance for Americans between the ages of forty and forty-nine is $105,500, the median account balance is

---

[23] The Pew Charitable Trusts. November 8, 2023. "Public Retirement Systems Need Sustainable Policies to Navigate Volatile Financial Markets" https://www.pewtrusts.org/en/research-and-analysis/issue-briefs/2023/11/public-retirement-systems-need-sustainable-policies-to-navigate-volatile-financial-markets

much lower. The median, which separates half of accounts with higher balances and half with lower balances, is just $34,100.[24]

Also, if you have changed jobs over the years, track down any benefits from your past employers. You might have an IRA here or a 401(k) there; keep track of those so you can pull them together and look at those assets when you're ready to look at establishing sources of retirement income.

## Do You Have ...

- Life insurance?
- Annuities?
- Long-term care insurance?
- Any passive income sources?
- Stock and bond portfolios?
- Liquid assets? (What's in your bank account?)
- Alternative investments?
- Rental properties?

If you are going through the work of sitting with a financial professional, it's important to look at your full retirement income picture and pull together *all* your assets, no matter how big or small. From the free insurance policy offered at your bank to the sizable investment in your brother-in-law's modestly successful furniture store, you want to have a good idea of where your money is.

I will never forget this one time we put together a plan for a couple. We'll call them Jerry and Kathy. They had never really taken inventory of their assets, nor done any type of planning to know if they were on track.

As we were going along, I could see Kathy kind of fidgeting in her chair. She was starting to look uncomfortable, almost like she had to go to the bathroom but didn't want to interrupt the

---

24 Cheyenne DeVon. CNBC. July 13, 2023. "Here's how much Americans in their 40s have in their 401(k)s" https://www.cnbc.com/2023/07/13/fidelity-how-much-americans-in-their-40s-have-in-their-401ks.html

meeting. So, I asked her if everything was all right. She couldn't hold it in anymore, and she started crying.

I was a little puzzled because everything we had looked at showed that they were going to be in great shape. I asked what was wrong and she said, "I just cannot believe this. We have worked so hard, and I cannot believe that what you are telling me is that we are millionaires."

She had no idea, and nobody had told her before. She had never added up the bank accounts, 401(k)s, investment accounts, savings bonds, home equity, etc. All those years of struggle and sacrifice for a tomorrow that was so far away were finally paying off. She was struck by that feeling of accomplishment, and seeing it all coming together was an emotional moment for her. It was such a great moment to be able to share with her and Jerry.

# Retirement Income Needs

How much income will you need in retirement? How do you determine that? A lot of people work toward a random number, thinking, "If I can just have a million dollars, I'll be comfortable in retirement!" Don't get me wrong; it is possible to save up a lot of money and then retire in the hopes you can keep your monthly expenses lower than some set estimation. But I think this carries a general risk of running out of money. Instead, I work with my clients to find out their current and projected income needs and then work from there to see how we might cover any gaps between what they have and what they want.

## Goals and Dreams

I like to start with your pie in the sky. Do you find yourself planning for your vacations more thoroughly than you do your retirement? Maybe it's because planning a vacation is less stressful: Having a week at the beach go awry is, well, a walk on the beach compared to running out of money in retirement.

Whatever the case, perhaps it would be better if you thought of your retirement as a vacation in and of itself — no clocking in, no boss, no overtime. If you felt unlimited by financial strain, what would you do?

Would an endless vacation for you mean Paris and Rome? Would it mean mentoring at children's clubs or serving at the local soup kitchen? Or maybe it would mean deepening your ties to those immediately around you — neighbors, friends, and family. Maybe it would mean more time to take part in the hobbies and activities you love. Have you been considering a second (or even third) act as a small-business owner, turning a hobby or passion into a revenue source?

This is your time to daydream and answer the question: If you could do anything, what would you do?

After that, it's a matter of putting a dollar amount on it. What are the costs of round-the-world travel? One couple I know said their highest priority in retirement was being able to take each of their grandchildren on a cross-country vacation every year. That's a pretty specific goal — one that is reasonably easy to nail down a budget for.

One of my favorite goal-planning experiences was with Tim and Sue. They had big plans of what they wanted to do, so it was fun to figure out what the finances would need to look like to make it happen.

They were getting ready to retire in a few months, and they planned to go on a big African safari while using up their paid time off at work. Then, they were going to sell their house, which was on a canal that was only a couple of minutes by boat to Lake Huron. After that, they eventually wanted to take that equity and buy a home in a big Florida retirement community where they didn't have to deal with cold winters. They wanted to be in a place with a lot of social happenings and drive a golf cart around. But before they were to settle down in the Sunshine State, they wanted to buy a motorhome and travel North America.

They are currently in Alaska in their motorhome that looks like something Kenny Chesney or the Red Hot Chili Peppers would tour in. I have to say, it is so much fun to follow their adventures online.

## Current Budget

Compiling a current expense report is one of the trickiest pieces of retirement preparation. Many people assume the expenses of their lives in retirement will be lower. After all, there will be no drive to work, no need for a formal wardrobe, and — perhaps most impactful of all — no more saving for retirement!

Yet, we often underestimate our daily spending habits. That's why I typically ask my clients to bring in their bank statements for the past year — they are reflective of your *actual* spending, not just what you think you're spending.

One way to find a rough estimate of what you'll spend in retirement is to go off of your current income and back out things like your retirement savings or work-related deductions.

If your bank balance is growing by $500 per month, we would back that out as well. The following would involve some work, but if you wanted to get an idea of what your true expenses are before you decide to retire, pretend you are already retired for twelve months. Do the things you are planning on doing, if possible; cut out the things you plan to cut out, if any; and write it all down. There is no better way to feel confident that you have the right number than by tracking it.

I can't count the number of times I have sat with a couple, asked them about their spending, and heard them throw out a number that seemed incredibly low. When I ask them where the number came from, they usually say they estimated based on their total bills. Yet, our spending is so much more than our mortgage, utilities, cable, phone, car, grocery, or credit card bills.

"What about clothes?" I ask, "Or dining out? What about gifts and coffees and last-minute birthday cards?" That's when the lights come on.

This is why I suggest collecting a year's worth of information. There is usually no such thing as a one-time purchase. Did you buy new furniture? Even if that is a rarity, do you think that will be the last time you *ever* buy furniture?

It is quite common for people that once they write down their expenses, they are surprised to see that they spend so much money on one area. Gasoline for example is something people just buy when the tank is low and don't always budget it. But when you total all those weekend road trips and commuting it can be a surprise. Groceries are another one that can catch people off guard.

Another hefty expense is spending on the kids. Many of the couples I work with are quick to help their adult children, whether it's something like letting them live in the basement, paying for college, babysitting, paying an occasional bill, or contributing to a grandchild's college fund. Research concluded that 54 percent of those in the Gen Z and millennial age groups lean on parents for financial support. Among those, 23 percent are heavily supported by parents.[25]

My clients sometimes protest that what they do for their grown children can stop in retirement. They don't *need* to help. But I get it. Parents like to feel needed. And, while you never want to neglect saving for retirement in favor of taking on financial risks (like your child's student debt), the parents who help their adult children do so in part because it helps them feel fulfilled.

When it comes down to expenses, including (and especially) spending on your family, don't make your initial calculations based on what you *could* whittle your budget down to if you *had* to. Instead, start from where you are. Who wants to live off a bare-bones bank account in retirement?

---

[25] Experian. June 27, 2023. "Most Gen Zers and millennials still rely on parents for financial support and feel ashamed asking for help" https://www.experianplc.com/newsroom/press-releases/2023/most-gen-zers-and-millennials-still-rely-on-parents-for-financial-support-and-feel-ashamed-asking-for-help

# Other Expenses

Once you have nailed down your current budget and your dreams or goals for retirement, there are a few other outstanding pieces to think about — some expenses many people don't take the time to consider before making and executing a plan. But I'm assuming you want to get it right, so let's take a look.

## Housing

Do you know where you want to live in retirement? This makes up a substantial piece of your income puzzle — since the typical American household owns a home, and it's generally their largest asset.

Some people prefer to live right where they are for as long as they can. Others have been waiting for retirement to pull the trigger on an ambitious move, like purchasing a new house or even downsizing. Whatever your plans and whatever your reasons, there are quite a few things to consider.

### *Mortgage*

Do you still have a mortgage? What may have been a nice tax boon in your working years could turn into a financial burden in your retirement. After all, when you are on a limited income, a mortgage is just one more bill sapping your financial strength. It is something to put some thought into, whether you plan to age in place or are considering moving to your dream home, buying a house out of state, or living in a retirement community.

### *Upkeep and Taxes*

A house without a mortgage still requires annual taxes. While it's tempting to think of this as a once-a-year expense, when you have limited earning potential, your annual tax bill might be something into which you should put a little more forethought.

The costs of homeownership aren't just monetary. When you find yourself dealing with more house than you need, it can drain your time and energy. From keeping clutter at bay to keeping the lawn mower running, upkeep can be extensive and expensive. For some, that's a challenge they heartily accept and can comfortably take on. For others, the idea of yard work or cleaning an area larger than they need feels foolish.

For instance, Peggy discovered after her knee replacement that most of her house was inaccessible to her when she was laid up.

"It felt ridiculous to pay someone else to dust and vacuum a house I was only living in 40 percent of!"

### *Practicality and Adaptability*

Erik and Marla are looking to retire within the next two decades. They just sold their old three-bedroom ranch-style house. Their twins are in high school, and the couple has wanted to "upgrade" for years. Now they live in a gorgeous 1940s three-story house with all the kitchen space they ever wanted, five sprawling bedrooms, and a library and media room for themselves and their children. Within months of moving in, the couple realized a house perfect for their active teens would no longer be perfect for them in five to fifteen years.

"We are paying the mortgage for this house, but we've started saving for the next one," said Marla, "because who wants to climb two flights of stairs to their bedroom when they're seventy-eight?"

Others I know have encountered a similar situation in their personal lives. After a health crisis, one couple found the luxurious tub for two they toiled to install had become a specter of a bad slip and a potential safety risk. It's important to think through what your physical reality could be. I always emphasize to my clients that they should plan for whatever their long-term future might hold, but it's amazing how many people don't give it much thought.

***Contracts and Regulations***

If you are looking into a cross-country move, be aware of new tax tables or local ordinances in the area where you are looking to move. After all, you don't want to experience sticker shock when looking at downsizing or reducing your bills in retirement.

Along the same lines, if you are moving into a retirement community, be sure to look at the fine print. What happens if you must move into a different situation for long-term care? Will you be penalized? Will you be responsible for replacing your slot in the community? What are all the fees, and what do they cover?

# Inflation

As I write this in 2024, America has experienced a wave of inflation following a lengthy period of low inflation. Inflation zoomed to 9.1 percent in June 2022, its highest mark since November 1981.[26] By August of 2024, the inflation rate decreased to 2.5 percent.[27] Consequently, inflation dropped to a three-year low in August 2024 after reaching a forty-year high in 2022 — quite the roller coaster.

Core inflation is yet another measurement that excludes goods with prices that tend to be more volatile, such as food and energy costs. Core inflation for a twelve-month period ending in November 2023 was 4.0 percent. It so happened that energy prices decreased 5.4 percent over that timeframe.[28]

However, inflation isn't a one-time bump; it has a cumulative effect. Again, that can impact the price of groceries more than other goods. Even with relatively low inflation over the past few decades, an item you bought in 1997 for $2 will cost

---

[26] Trading Economics. 2024. "United States Inflation Rate" https://tradingeconomics.com/united-states/inflation-cpi

[27] Ibid.

[28] U.S. Inflation Calculator. 2024. "United States Core Inflation Rates (1957-2024)" https://www.usinflationcalculator.com/inflation/united-states-core-inflation-rates/

about $3.92 today.[29] Want to go to a show? A $20 ticket in 1997 would cost $45.18 in 2024.[30]

What if we hit a stretch in retirement like the late seventies and early eighties, when annual inflation rates of 10 percent became the norm? It may be wise to consider some extra padding in your retirement income plan to account for any potential increase in inflation in the future.

## Shrinkflation

Another important yet often overlooked factor to consider is called "shrinkflation." Essentially a form of hidden inflation, shrinkflation signifies a reduction in packaging while retaining a similar price as before.

For example, as you walk down a grocery store aisle, you spot your favorite pickles. The jar still costs the same — roughly $5 — and you add it to your cart. Then you get home, and the container seems different after digging out a few crispy dills. You examine the jar and discover it contains fewer ounces than previous jars you purchased. However, you paid roughly the same price for your pickles.

Now, move over to the aisle featuring salty snacks. You might notice a sale on a certain brand of chips, though you must buy three or four bags to receive a discount promoted by the store. You decide to purchase that many bags to capitalize on the lower price. When you get home, you notice the packaging is smaller than you anticipated. The deal you accepted may not have been as thrifty as you perceived.

Shrinkflation can be a way for companies to quietly boost (or retain) profit margins without having to change much else — essentially, they are simply charging the same price for less

---

[29] in2013dollars.com. 2024. "$2 in 1997 is worth $3.92 today" https://www.in2013dollars.com/us/inflation/1997?amount=2

[30] in2013dollars.com. 2024. "Admission to movies, theaters, and concerts priced at $20 in 1997 ->$45.18 in 2024" https://www.in2013dollars.com/Admission-to-movies,-theaters,-and-concerts/price-inflation

product. Companies do this because customers are more likely to spot price increases than size reductions. However, research has also shown that these shrinkflation tactics can backfire into negative consumer perceptions of their brands once they come to light. Who wants to pay the same for less, especially when they have already grown accustomed to getting more for their money's worth?[31]

## Aging

Also, in the expense category, think about longevity. We all hope to age gracefully. However, it's important to face the prospect of aging with a sense of realism.

For many families, the elephant in the room is long-term care. No one wants to admit they will likely need it, but estimates indicate almost 70 percent of us will.[32] Aging is a significant piece of retirement income planning because you'll want to figure out how to set aside money for your care, either at home or away from it. The more comfortable you get with discussing your wishes and plans with your loved ones, the easier it can be to plan financially.

I denote health care and potential long-term care costs in more detail elsewhere in this book, but suffice it to say nursing home care tends to be very expensive and typically isn't something you get to choose when you will need.

It isn't just the costs of long-term care that pose a concern in living longer. It's also about covering the possible costs of everything else associated with living longer. For instance, if Henry retires from his job as a biochemical engineer at age sixty-five, perhaps he plans to have a very decent income for twenty years until he turns eighty-five. But what if he lives until

---

[31] Daniel Liberto. Investopedia. November 16, 2023. "Shrinkflation: What It Is, Reasons for It, How to Spot It"
https://www.investopedia.com/terms/s/shrinkflation.asp

[32] Moll Law Group. 2024. "The Cost of Long-Term Care"
https://www.molllawgroup.com/the-cost-of-long-term-care.html

he's ninety-five? That's a whole third — ten years — more of personal income he will need.

## Putting It All Together

Whew! So, you have pulled together what you have, and you have a pretty good idea of where you want to be. Now, you and your financial professional can go about the work of arranging what assets you *have* to cover what you *need* — and how you might try to cover any gaps.

Like the proverbial man in the Bible who built his house on a rock, I like to help my clients figure out how to cover their day-to-day living expenses — their needs — with insurance and other guaranteed income sources like pensions and Social Security.

We create a customized Retire Boldly plan for each of our clients. It consists of five main elements: Income Planning, Investment Planning, Tax Planning, Legacy, and Healthcare. It will provide an analysis of each planning characteristic and how they interact.

What you do with your investments directly impacts your taxes. What you do with your taxes directly impacts your legacy. Your income plan consists of what you decide to do with your Social Security or pension. Therefore, the timing of when you need to draw down on your investments or pay taxes on your income and assets are all affected.

These decisions should not be made in isolation., We'll take all of those interactions into consideration to make things as simple as possible. The recommendations of what to invest in or what insurance you may or may not need stem from the plan. Far too many times, we see people and other "financial professionals" start with the latter and jump into what might be a good "product" or investment without knowing if, how, or when it actually fits into your situation.

Again, you should keep in mind there isn't one single financial vehicle, asset, or source to fill all your needs, and that's okay. One of the challenges of planning for your income in retirement concerns figuring out what products and strategies to use. You can release some of that stress when you accept the fact you will probably need a diverse portfolio — potentially with bonds, stocks, insurance, and other income sources — not just one massive money pile.

One way to help shore up your income gaps is by working with your financial professional and a qualified tax advisor to help mitigate your tax exposure. If you have a 401(k) or IRA, a tax advisor in your corner may be able to help you figure out how and when to take distributions from your account in a way that doesn't push you into a higher tax bracket. You might also learn of ways to use tax-advantaged bonds more effectively. Effective tax planning isn't necessarily about "adding" to your income. Especially regarding retirement, it's less about what you make than it is about what you keep. Paying a lower tax bill keeps more money in your pocket, which is where you want it when it comes to retirement income.

Now you can look at ways to cover your remaining retirement goals. Are there products like long-term care insurance specific to a certain kind of expense you anticipate? Is there a particular asset you want to use for your "play" money — money for trips and gifts for the grandkids? Is there any way you can portion off money for those charitable legacy plans?

Once you have analyzed your income wants, needs, and the assets necessary to realistically cover them, you may have a gap. The masterstroke of a competent financial professional will be to help you figure out how you will cover that gap. Will you need to cut out a round of golf a week? Maybe skip the new car? Or will you need to take more substantial action?

One way to cover an income gap is to consider working longer or even part-time before retirement and even after that magical calendar date. This may not be the best "plan" for you; disabilities, work demands, and physical or emotional limitations can hinder the best-laid plans to continue working. However, if it is physically possible for you, this is one considerable way to help your assets last for more than one reason.

In fact, 55 percent of Americans responding to a survey reported they plan to work part-time after retiring, while 15 percent expect compensation from work to be their primary source of retirement income.[33]

When you're retired, you no longer have an employer paying you a steady check. It is up to you to make sure you have saved and planned for the income you need.

It still surprises me how many people continue to work because they just have no idea if they can retire. Some people are afraid of change, and I understand that. Some people are confused and don't know where to turn. Some people don't know who to trust. Maybe if they had a bad experience someplace, they think that must be how all financial advisors are.

One of the most rewarding things we get to do is when we meet with someone and they tell us that they would love to retire today if they could, but say, "that's not realistic." And then, we work with them to create their Retire Boldly plan, where they find out what is possible, and they can clearly see how. It can be a life-changing moment!

Then there is the scenario where we do the same planning process for someone who said they were a few years away from retirement. Then in our next review meeting together, they surprise us by telling us they changed their mind and are retiring now because they had reevaluated their priorities. Since the plan showed it was possible, they decided they would retire earlier than they originally planned.

A more recent trend I have seen is people that might be working in a job they hate or are just feeling burnt out by it and are only sticking it out for the paycheck. Then when seeing their Retire Boldly plan, they sometimes find it possible to retire

---

33 Kerry Hannon. Yahoo! Finance. July 15, 2023. "Future retirees plan to work longer, partly due to savings shortfalls" https://finance.yahoo.com/news/future-retirees-plan-to-work-longer-partly-due-to-savings-shortfalls-160038419.html

from their job and go to work doing something they are passionate about, get energized by, and find renewed purpose. Even if that new job doesn't pay as much, it may still be worth it!

CHAPTER 5

# Social Security

Social Security is often the foundation of retirement income. Backed by the strength of the U.S. Treasury, it provides perhaps the most dependable paycheck you will have in retirement.

From the time you collect your first paycheck from the job that made you a bona fide taxpayer (for me, it was stocking shelves at the local grocery store in the small town I grew up in), you are paying into the grand old Social Security system. What grew and developed out of the pressures of the Great Depression has become one of the most popular government programs in the country, and if you pay in for the equivalent of ten years or more, you, too, can benefit from the Social Security program.

Now, before we get into the nitty-gritty of Social Security, I'd like to address a current concern: Will Social Security still be there for you when you reach retirement age?

## The Future of Social Security

This question is ever-present as headlines trumpet an underfunded Social Security program alongside the sea of baby boomers retiring in droves and the comparatively smaller pool of younger people who are funding the system.

The Social Security Administration itself acknowledges this concern as each Social Security statement now contains a link to its website (ssa.gov) and a page entitled, "Will Social Security Be There For Me?"

Just a reminder, as if you needed one, that nothing in life is guaranteed. Additionally, depending on who you're listening to, Social Security funds may run low before 2034, thanks to the financial instability and government spending that accompanied the 2020 COVID-19 pandemic.

Before you get too discouraged, though, here are a few thoughts to keep you going:

- Even if the program is only paying 75 to 78 cents on the dollar for scheduled benefits, this is notably not zero.
- The Social Security Administration has made changes in the distant and near past to help protect the fund's solvency, including increasing retirement ages and striking certain filing strategies.
- There are many changes Congress could make, and lawmakers routinely discuss ideas for amending the system, such as further increasing full retirement age and eligibility.
- One thing no one is seriously discussing? Reneging on current obligations to retirees or the soon-to-retire.

Take heart. The real answer to the question, "Will Social Security be there for me?" is still yes.

This question is important to consider when you look at how much we, as a nation, rely on this program. Did you know Social Security benefits replace about 39 percent of a person's original income when they retire?[34]

If you ask me, that's a pretty significant piece of your retirement income puzzle.

Another caveat? You may not realize this, but no one can legally "advise" you about your Social Security benefits.

---

34 Center on Budget and Policy Priorities. May 31, 2024. "Top Ten Facts About Social Security" https://www.cbpp.org/sites/default/files/atoms/files/8-8-16socsec.pdf

"But, Russ," you may be thinking, "isn't that part of what you do? And what about that nice gentleman at the Social Security Administration office I spoke with on the phone?"

Don't get me wrong. Social Security Administration employees know their stuff. They are trained to understand policies and programs, and they are usually pretty quick to tell you what you can and cannot do. However, the government specifically stipulates that because Social Security is a benefit you alone have paid into and earned, your Social Security decisions are *also* yours alone.

When it comes to financial professionals, we can't push you in any direction, but — there's a big but here — working with a well-informed financial professional is still incredibly handy for your Social Security decisions. Why? Because someone who's worth their salt will know what withdrawal strategies might pertain to your specific situation and will ask questions that can help you determine what you are looking for when it comes to your Social Security.

For instance, some people want the highest possible monthly benefit. Others want to start their benefits early, and not always because of financial need. I heard about one man who called in to start his Social Security payments the day he qualified just because he liked to think of it as the government paying back a debt it owed him, and he enjoyed the feeling of receiving a check from Uncle Sam.

Whatever your reasons, questions, or feelings regarding Social Security, the decision is yours alone, but working with a financial professional can help you put your options in perspective by showing you — both with industry knowledge and with proprietary software or planning processes — where your benefits fit into your overall strategy for retirement income.

# Full Retirement Age

When it comes to Social Security, it seems like many people only think so far as "yes." They don't take the time to understand the various options available. Instead, because it is common knowledge you can begin your benefits at age sixty-two, that's what many of us do. While more people are opting to delay taking benefits, age sixty-two is still a popular age to start.[35]

Some people fail to understand that starting benefits early may leave significant money on the table. You see, the Social Security Administration bases your monthly benefit on two factors: your earnings history and your full retirement age (FRA).

From your earnings history, the SSA pulls the thirty-five years you made the most money and uses a mathematical indexing formula to figure out a monthly average from those years. If you paid into the system for less than thirty-five years, every year you didn't pay in will be counted as a zero.

Once they have calculated what your monthly earnings would be at FRA, the government then calculates what to put on your check based on how close you are to FRA. FRA was originally set at sixty-five, but as the population aged and lifespans lengthened, the government shifted FRA later and later, based on an individual's year of birth. Check out the following chart to see when you will reach FRA.[36]

---

[35] Emily Brandon. Erica Sandberg. U.S. News & World Report. August 14, 2023. "The Most Popular Ages to Collect Social Security" https://money.usnews.com/money/retirement/social-security/articles/the-most-popular-ages-to-collect-social-security

[36] Social Security Administration. 2024. "Starting Your Retirement Benefits Early" https://www.ssa.gov/benefits/retirement/planner/agereduction.html

| Age to Receive Full Social Security Benefits* | |
|---|---|
| *(Called "full retirement age" [FRA] or "normal retirement age.")* | |
| Year of Birth* | FRA |
| 1937 or earlier | 65 |
| 1938 | 65 and 2 months |
| 1939 | 65 and 4 months |
| 1940 | 65 and 6 months |
| 1941 | 65 and 8 months |
| 1942 | 65 and 10 months |
| 1943-1954 | 66 |
| 1955 | 66 and 2 months |
| 1956 | 66 and 4 months |
| 1957 | 66 and 6 months |
| 1958 | 66 and 8 months |
| 1959 | 66 and 10 months |
| 1960 and later | 67 |
| **If you were born on January 1 of any year, you should refer to the previous year. (If you were born on the 1st of the month, we figure your benefit [and your full retirement age] as if your birthday was in the previous month.)*[37] | |

When you reach FRA, you are eligible to receive 100 percent of whatever the Social Security Administration calculates as your full monthly benefit.

Starting at age sixty-two, for every year before FRA you claim benefits, your monthly check is reduced by 5 percent or more.

---

37 Social Security Administration. 2024. "Normal Retirement Age" https://www.ssa.gov/oact/progdata/nra.html

Conversely, for every year you delay taking benefits past FRA, your monthly benefit increases by 8 percent (until age seventy — after that, there is no monetary advantage to delaying Social Security benefits). While your circumstances and needs may vary, a lot of financial professionals still urge people to at least consider delaying until they reach age seventy.

Why wait?[38]

| **Taking benefits early could affect your monthly check by ____.** | | | | | | | | |
|---|---|---|---|---|---|---|---|---|
| 62 | 63 | 64 | 65 | 66 | FRA 67 | 68 | 69 | 70 |
| -30% | -25% | -20% | -13.3% | -6.7% | 0 | +8% | +16% | +24% |

39

## My Social Security

If you are over thirty, you have probably received a notice from the Social Security Administration telling you to activate something called "My Social Security." This is a handy way to learn more about your particular benefit options, keep track of your earnings record, and calculate the benefits you have accrued over the years.

Essentially, My Social Security is an online account you can activate to see your personal Social Security picture. You can access this information at www.ssa.gov/myaccount. This can be extremely helpful when it comes to planning for retirement income and figuring out the difference between your anticipated income and anticipated expenses.

---

[38] Social Security Administration. 2024. "Retirement Benefits" https://www.ssa.gov/pubs/EN-05-10035.pdf

[39] Social Security Administration. 2024. "Effect of Early or Delayed Retirement on Retirement Benefits" https://www.ssa.gov/oact/ProgData/ar_drc.html

## COLA

Social Security is a largely guaranteed piece of the retirement puzzle: If you get a statement that reads you should expect $1,000 a month, you can be sure you will receive $1,000 a month. However, there is one variable detail, and that is something called the cost-of-living adjustment (COLA).

The COLA is an increase in your monthly check meant to address inflation in everyday life. After all, your expenses will likely continue to experience inflation in retirement, but you will no longer have the opportunity for raises, bonuses, or promotions you had when you were working. Instead, Social Security receives an annual cost-of-living increase tied to the Department of Labor's Consumer Price Index for Urban Wage Earners and Clerical Workers (CPI-W). If the CPI-W measurement shows inflation rose a certain amount for regular goods and services, then Social Security recipients will see that reflected in their COLA.

COLA adjustments have climbed as high as 14.3 percent (1980), and in 2023, they reached 8.7 percent — the largest increase in more than forty years. In a no- or low-inflation environment (such as in 2010, 2011, and 2016), Social Security recipients will not receive an adjustment.[40] The 2024 adjustment decreased to 3.2 percent.[41] Some view the COLA as a perk, bump, or bonus, but in reality, it works more like this: Your mom sends you to the store with $2.50 for a gallon of milk. Milk costs exactly $2.50. The next week, you go back with that same amount, but it is now $2.52 for a gallon, so you go back to Mom, and she gives you 2 cents. You aren't bringing home more milk — it just costs more money.

The COLA is less about "making more money" and more about keeping seniors' purchasing power from eroding when inflation is a big factor. Still, don't let that detract from your

---

[40] Social Security Administration. 2024. "Cost-Of-Living Adjustments" https://www.ssa.gov/oact/cola/colaseries.html

[41] Social Security Administration. 2024. "Cost-of-Living Adjustment (COLA) Information for 2024" https://www.ssa.gov/cola/

enthusiasm about COLAs. After all, what if Mom's solution was: "Here's the same $2.50. Try to find pennies from somewhere else to get that milk!"?

## Spousal Benefits

We've talked about FRA, but another big Social Security decision involves spousal benefits.

If you or your spouse has a long stretch of zeros in your earnings history — perhaps if one of you stayed home for years, caring for children or sick relatives — you may want to consider filing for spousal benefits instead of filing on your own earnings history. A spousal benefit can be up to 50 percent of the primary wage earner's benefit at full retirement age.

To begin drawing a spousal benefit, you must be at least sixty-two years old, and the primary wage earner must have already filed for their benefit. While there are reductions for taking spousal benefits early, you cannot earn credits for delaying past full retirement age.[42]

As I wrote, the spousal benefit can be a big deal for those who don't have a very long pay history, but it's important to weigh your own earned benefits against the option of withdrawing based on a fraction of your spouse's benefits.

To look at how this could play out, let's use a hypothetical couple: Mary Jane, who is sixty, and Peter, who is sixty-two.

Let's say Peter's benefit at FRA — in his case, sixty-seven — would be $1,600. If Peter begins his benefits right now (five years before FRA), his monthly check will be $1,120. If Mary Jane begins taking spousal benefits in two years at the earliest date possible, her monthly benefits will $560 per month.

What if Peter and Mary Jane both wait until FRA? At sixty-seven, Peter begins taking his full benefit of $1,600 a month. Two years later, when she reaches age sixty-seven, Mary Jane will qualify for $800 a month (half of Peter's FRA benefit). By

---

[42] Social Security Administration. 2024. "Family Benefits" https://www.ssa.gov/family

waiting until FRA, the couple's monthly benefit goes from $1,680 to $2,400.

What if Peter delays until age seventy to get his maximum possible benefit? For each year past FRA he delays, his monthly benefits increase by 8 percent. This means that at seventy, he could file for a monthly benefit of $1,984. However, delayed retirement credits do not affect spousal benefits, so as soon as Peter files at seventy, Mary Jane would also file (at age sixty-eight) for her maximum benefit of $800, so their highest possible combined monthly check is $2,784.[43]

When it comes to your Social Security benefits, you obviously will want to consider whether a monthly check based on a fraction of your spouse's earnings will be comparable to or larger than your own earnings history.

## Divorced Spouses

There are a few considerations for those of us who have gone through a divorce. If you 1) were married for ten years or more *and* 2) have since been divorced for at least two years *and* 3) are unmarried *and* 4) your ex-spouse qualifies to begin Social Security, you qualify for a spousal benefit based on your ex-spouse's earnings history at FRA. A divorced spousal benefit is different from a married spousal benefit in one way: You don't have to wait for your ex-spouse to file before you can file yourself.[44]

For instance, Charles and Moira were married for fifteen years before their divorce, when he was thirty-six and she was forty. Moira has been remarried for twenty years, and although Charles briefly remarried, his second marriage ended after a few years. Charles' benefits are largely calculated based on his many years of volunteering in schools, meaning his personal monthly benefit is close to zero.

---

[43] Social Security Administration. 2024. "Benefits for Spouses" https://www.ssa.gov/OACT/quickcalc/spouse.html#calculator

[44] Social Security Administration. 2024. "Family Benefits" https://www.ssa.gov/family

Although Moira has deferred her retirement (opting to delay benefits until she is seventy), Charles can begin taking benefits calculated from Moira's work history at FRA as early as sixty-two. However, he will also have the option of waiting until FRA to collect the maximum, which is 50 percent of Moira's earned monthly benefit at her FRA.

### Widowed Spouses

If your marriage ended with the death of your spouse, you might claim a benefit for your spouse's earned income as their widow/widower called a survivor's benefit. Unlike spousal benefits or divorced benefits, if your spouse dies, you can claim their full benefit. Also, unlike spousal benefits, you can begin taking income when you turn sixty if you need to. However, as with other benefit options, your monthly check will be permanently reduced for withdrawing benefits before FRA.

If your spouse began taking benefits before they died, you can't delay withdrawing your survivor's benefits to get delayed credits. The Social Security Administration maintains you can only get as much from a survivor's benefit as your deceased spouse might have received had they lived.[45]

## Taxes, Taxes, Taxes

With Social Security — as with everything — it is important to consider taxes. It may be surprising, but your Social Security benefits are not tax-free. Despite having been taxed to accrue those benefits in the first place, you may have to pay Uncle Sam income taxes on up to 85 percent of your Social Security.

The Social Security Administration figures these taxes using what they call "the provisional income formula." Your provisional income formula differs from the gross income you use for your regular income taxes. Instead, to find out how

---

[45] Social Security Administration. 2024. "What you could get from Survivor benefits" https://www.ssa.gov/survivor/amount

much of your Social Security benefit is taxable, the Social Security Administration calculates it this way:

*Provisional Income =*
*Gross Income + Nontaxable Interest + ½ of Social Security*

See that piece about nontaxable interest? That generally means interest from government bonds and notes. It surprises many people that although you may not pay taxes on those assets, their income will count against you when it comes to Social Security taxation.

Once you have figured out your provisional income (also called "combined income"), you can use the following chart to figure out your Social Security taxes. [46]

| **Taxes on Social Security** | | |
|---|---|---|
| *Provisional Income = Gross Income + Nontaxable Interest + ½ of Social Security* | | |
| If you are ____ and your provisional income is____, then ... | | Uncle Sam will tax ___ of your Social Security |
| Single | Married, filing jointly | |
| Less than $25,000 | Less than $32,000 | 0% |
| $25,000 to $34,000 | $32,000 to $44,000 | Up to 50% |
| More than $34,000 | More than $44,000 | Up to 85% |

[47]

[46] Motley Fool Staff. The Motley Fool. May 30, 2024. "How to Calculate Provisional Income" https://www.fool.com/investing/how-to-calculate/provisional-income/
[47] Ibid.

This is one more reason why working with financial and tax professionals may benefit you. They can help you look at your entire financial picture to make your overall retirement plan as tax-efficient as possible — including your Social Security benefit.

Did you happen to notice an income source that is NOT included in the calculation above? Qualified income from Roth IRAs is not part of the math. This is a significant missed opportunity for a lot of retirees who think they are always going to be stuck paying taxes on their Social Security.

It doesn't need to be this way (unless, of course, you have a large pension and adding in half your Social Security puts you above the top tier). For a lot of folks, putting as much money into a Roth IRA can be beneficial in general. Then add in the fact that the Roth IRA gives you the flexibility to pull out money tax-free when you need it. Those funds can potentially keep you from paying taxes on your Social Security.

This could mean as much as thousands of dollars per year that stay in your pocket. Over a thirty-year retirement, that can add up to a very meaningful amount.

## Working and Social Security: The Earnings Test

If you haven't reached FRA but you started your Social Security benefits and are still working, things get a little hairy.

Because you have started Social Security payments, the Social Security Administration will pay out your benefits (at that reduced rate, of course, because you haven't reached your FRA). Yet, because you are working, the organization must also withhold from your check to add to your benefits, which you are already collecting. See how this complicates matters?

To address the situation, the government has what is called the earnings test. For 2024, you can earn up to $23,400 without it affecting your Social Security check if you're younger than full retirement age. But, for every $2 you earn past that amount, the Social Security Administration will withhold $1. The earnings test loosens in the year of your FRA; if you are reaching FRA in 2024, you can earn up to $62,160 before you run into the earnings test, and the government only withholds $1 for every $3 past that amount.

The month you reach FRA, you are no longer subject to any earnings withholding. For instance, if you are still working and will turn sixty-seven on December 28, 2024, you would only have to worry about the earnings test until December, and then you can ignore it entirely. Keep in mind, the money the government withholds from your Social Security benefits while you are working before FRA will be tacked back onto your benefits check after FRA.[48]

There are Social Security calculators out there that will help you determine how you can help maximize what you get from the Social Security Administration. The part that is missing from the math many times is "opportunity cost." Opportunity cost is a term from economics class that refers to missed opportunity or value that could have been created if you had that money in hand earlier.

In other words, what value is gained by you having that money in hand at sixty-two instead of waiting for a future date like age sixty-seven? Every dollar you have in hand at sixty-two might mean that that's a dollar you don't need to take out of your investments and can leave in there to grow.

I'm not saying everyone must take their Social Security at sixty-two. But I am saying that the growth on having the money in hand needs to be part of the equation. We pay for very robust planning software to be able to do this for our clients. I believe it's a step that sets us apart from others.

---

[48] Social Security Administration. 2024. "Receiving Benefits While Working"
https://www.ssa.gov/benefits/retirement/planner/whileworking.html

# Railroad Retirement Benefits

The Railroad Retirement Act was established in 1934 to address concerns about existing pension programs' ability to provide former railroad employees with old-age benefits.[49] The Act continues to provide benefits to retired and disabled workers and their dependents based on their length of employment in the industry. Although there are similarities to Social Security, there are considerable differences, which include payment amounts, eligibility age, and taxation obligations.

Like Social Security, Railroad Retirement Benefits (RRB) are funded from payroll taxes of current employees and employers. Also, retirees receive both types of benefits as a monthly check. RRBs use the same formula to calculate COLAs as Social Security.

The differences between the two retirement programs are intricate. The average monthly RRB payment is more generous than Social Security because railroad workers pay higher taxes into the program. Another major difference is the age at which railroad workers are eligible to begin collecting benefits: A railroad worker with thirty or more years of service is eligible for full benefits at age sixty without a reduction.

The taxation of RRBs is more complex than Social Security payments. To determine the tax, RRBs include two components:

- Tier I benefits resemble Social Security, a private pension, or a combination of both
- Tier II benefits are similar to a private pension[50]

The portion of the Tier I benefit equivalent to Social Security is taxed the same way as Social Security benefits, but the portion not equivalent is fully taxable. Regarding the Tier II, a

---

[49] U.S. Railroad Retirement Board. January 2024. "Agency Overview" https://www.rrb.gov/OurAgency/AgencyOverview

[50] Kurt Woock. NerdWallet. February 7, 2024. "Railroad Retirement Board: What It Is, How It Works" https://www.nerdwallet.com/article/investing/social-security/what-is-the-railroad-retirement-board

portion is always taxable and subject to ordinary income tax rates.[51]

[51] True Tamplin. Finance Strategists. September 7, 2023. "Is Railroad Retirement Income Taxable?" https://www.financestrategists.com/retirement-planning/retirement-income-planning/is-railroad-retirement-income-taxable/

CHAPTER 6

# 401(k)s, IRAs, and Roth IRAs

Have you heard? Today's retirement is not your parents' retirement. You see, back in the day, it was pretty common to work for one company for the vast majority of your career and then retire with a gold watch and a pension.

The gold watch was a symbol of the quality time you had put in at that company, but the pension was more than a symbol. Instead, it was a guarantee — as solid as your employer — that they would repay your hard work with a certain amount of income in your old age. Did you see the caveat there? Your pension's guarantee was *as solid as your employer*. The problem was, what if your employer went under?

Companies that failed couldn't pay their retired employees' pensions, leading to financial challenges for many. Beginning in 1974 with Congress' passage of the Employee Retirement Income Security Act, federal legislation and regulations aimed at protecting retirees were everywhere. One piece of legislation included a relatively obscure section of the Internal Revenue Code, added in 1978 — Section 401(k), to be specific.

IRC section 401, subsection k, created tax advantages for employer-sponsored financial products, even if the main contributors were the employees themselves. Over the years, more employers took note, beginning an age of transition away from pensions and toward 401(k) plans. A 401(k) is a retirement account with certain tax benefits and restrictions on the investments or other financial products inside of it.

Essentially, 401(k)s and their individual retirement account (IRA) counterparts are "wrappers" that provide tax benefits around assets; typically, the assets that compose IRAs and 401(k)s are mutual funds, stock and bond mixes, and money market accounts. However, IRA and 401(k) contents are becoming more diverse these days, with some companies offering different kinds of annuity options within their plans.

Where pensions are defined-*benefit* plans, 401(k)s and IRAs are defined-*contribution* plans. The one-word change outlines the basic difference. Pensions spell out what you can expect to receive from the plan but not necessarily how much money it will take to fund those benefits. With 401(k)s, an employer sets a standard for how much they will contribute (if any), and you can be certain of what you are contributing. Still, there is no outline of what you can expect to receive in return for those contributions.

Modern employment looks very different. According to a 2024 report by Forbes, U.S. workers stay with their employers for a median of 4.1 years.[52] Participation in 401(k) plans appears solid. A study by Vanguard reported a record plan participation rate of 85 percent in 2023. Plans with automatic enrollment drew a 94 percent participation rate.[53]

Those statistics make it clear that 401(k) plans have replaced pensions at many companies and, for that matter, a gold watch.

If you are one of the folks with a pension, your retirement planning might be a little more rigid. This means you will collect a monthly amount that doesn't fluctuate, and that's pretty much it.

---

[52] Kristy Snyder. Cassie Bottorff. Forbes. May 17, 2023. "Key HR Statistics And Trends In 2024" https://www.forbes.com/advisor/business/hr-statistics-trends/

[53] Vanguard. 2023. "How America Saves 2024" https://institutional.vanguard.com/content/dam/inst/iig-transformation/insights/pdf/2024/has/how_america_saves_report_2024.pdf

However, there are still some decisions to make. You will need to determine which monthly option makes sense if you are married, as there are different survivor options. You may have a lump sum option available, which would allow you to forgo the monthly payments, roll over a lump sum amount to an IRA, and then just take distributions from there.

Sometimes people choose to take the lump sum option because they hear the stories of pension funds being underfunded or perhaps they want the asset to stay in their estate once they and their spouse pass. A monthly pension ends once both spouses are gone.

If there is anything to learn from this paradigm shift, it's that you must look out for yourself. Whether you have worked for a company for two years or twenty, you are still the one who has to look out for your own best interests. That holds doubly true when it comes to preparing for retirement. If you are one of the lucky ones who still has a pension, good for you. But for the rest of us, it is likely a 401(k) — or possibly one of its nonprofit- or government-sector counterparts, a 403(b) or 457 plan — is one of your biggest assets for retirement.

Some employers offer incentives to contribute to their company plans, like a company match. On that subject, I have one thing to say: *Do it!* Nothing in life is free, as they say, but a company match on your retirement funds is about as close to free money as it gets. If you can make the minimum to qualify for your company's match at all, go for it.

Now, it's likely that during our working years, we mostly "set and forget" our 401(k) funding. Because it is tax-advantaged, your employer is taking money from your paycheck — before taxes — and putting it into your plan for you. Maybe you were able to pick a selection of investments, or maybe your company only offers one choice of investment in your 401(k). Either way, while you are gainfully employed, your most impactful decision may just be the decision to continue funding your plan in the first place. But when you are ready to retire or move jobs, you have choices to make requiring a little more thought and care.

When you are ready to part ways with your job, you have a few options:

- Leave the money where it is
- Take the cash (and pay income taxes and perhaps a 10 percent additional federal tax if you are younger than age fifty-nine-and-one-half)
- Transfer the money to another employer plan (if the new plan allows)
- Roll the money over into a self-directed IRA

Now, these are just general options. You will have to decide — hopefully with the help of a financial professional — what's right for you. For instance, 401(k)s are typically pretty closely tied to the companies offering them, so when changing jobs, it may not always be possible to transfer a 401(k) to another 401(k). Leaving the money where it is may also be out of the question — some companies have direct cash payout or rollover policies once someone is no longer employed.

Also, remember what we mentioned earlier about how we change jobs more often these days? That means you likely have a 401(k) with your current company, but you may also have a string of retirement accounts trailing you from other jobs.

Having money in multiple places can make investment management more challenging. It can also be tougher to remember where your money is at. I met with someone once who had a letter from the Social Security Administration saying they had an old 401(k) someplace.

This person thought it was a scam and had ignored it in previous years. It turned out that after we called, he had $40,000 he didn't know about. The unfortunate part is that for the last twenty years, he didn't get any growth while it sat in an abandoned account.

When it comes to your retirement income, it's important to be able to pull together *all* your assets so you can examine what you have and where and then decide what you will do with it.

## Tax-Qualified, Tax-Preferred, Tax-Deferred ... Still TAXED

Financial media often cite IRAs and 401(k)s for their tax benefits. After all, with traditional plans, you put your money in pre-tax, and it hopefully grows for years — even decades — untaxed. That's why these accounts are called "tax-qualified" or "tax-deferred" assets. They aren't *tax-free!* Rarely does Uncle Sam allow business to continue without receiving his piece of the pie, and your retirement assets are no different. If you didn't pay taxes on the front end, you will pay taxes on the money you withdraw from these accounts in retirement. Don't get me wrong: This isn't an inherently good or bad thing; it's just the way it is. It's important to understand, though, for the sake of planning ahead.

In retirement, many people assume they will be in a lower tax bracket. As referenced in the Taxes chapter, for retirees with healthy balances in tax-deferred assets, their retirement marginal tax rate may be the same or even more than their pre-retirement rate. The timing involved with beginning Social Security or in shifting or converting funds out of tax-deferred assets is of strategic concern because of taxes owed on those assets.

Keep in mind, IRAs, 401(k)s, and their alternatives have a few limitations because of their special tax status. For one thing, the IRS sets limits on your contributions to these retirement accounts. If you are contributing to a 401(k) or an equivalent nonprofit or government plan, your annual contribution limit is $23,000 (as of 2024). If you are fifty or older, the IRS allows additional contributions, called "catch-up contributions," of up to $7,500 on top of the regular limit of $23,000. For an IRA, the limit is $7,000, with a catch-up limit of an additional $1,000.[54] Beginning in 2026, catch-up

[54] Fidelity. March 4, 2024. "IRA contribution limits for 2024" https://www.fidelity.com/learning-center/smart-money/ira-contribution-limits

contributions for individuals with income exceeding $145,000 must be transferred into a Roth IRA.[55]

Because their tax advantages come from their intended use as retirement income, withdrawing funds from these accounts before you turn fifty-nine-and-one-half can carry stiff penalties. In addition to fees your investment management company might charge, you will have to pay income tax *and* a 10 percent federal tax penalty, with a few exceptions.

The fifty-nine-and-one-half rule for retirement accounts is incredibly important to remember, especially when you're young. Younger workers are often tempted to cash out an IRA from a previous employer and then are surprised to find their checks missing 20 percent of the account value to income taxes, penalty taxes, and account fees.

Many millennials I see in my practice say that while they may be socking money away in their workplace retirement plan, it is often the *only* place they are saving. This could be problematic later because of the fifty-nine-and-one-half rule; what if you have an emergency? It is important to fund your retirement, but you need to have some liquid assets handy as emergency funds. This can help you avoid breaking into your retirement accounts and incurring taxes and penalties because of the fifty-nine-and-one-half rule.

## RMDs

Remember how we talked about the 401(k) or IRA being a "tax wrapper" for your funds? Well, eventually, Uncle Sam will want a bite of that candy bar. So, when you turn seventy-three, the government requires you to withdraw a portion of your account, which the IRS calculates based on the size of your account and your estimated lifespan. This required minimum

---

[55] Robert Powell. The Street. September 11, 2023. "Ask the Hammer: Catch-up Contributions Now Permitted Until 2026" https://www.thestreet.com/retirement-daily/ask-the-hammer/catch-up-contributions-now-permitted-until-2026

distribution (RMD) is the government's insurance it will collect some taxes from your earnings at some point. Because you didn't pay taxes on the front end, you will now pay income taxes on whatever you withdraw — including your RMDs.

Let me reiterate something I pointed out in the Longevity chapter. Beginning at age seventy-three, you are required to withdraw a certain minimum amount every year from your 401(k) or IRA, or else you will face a tax penalty on any RMD monies you should have withdrawn but didn't — and that's on top of income tax. The SECURE Act 2.0 reduced the penalty to 25 percent (from 50 percent). Timely corrections also can reduce the penalty to 10 percent.[56]

Even after you begin RMDs, you can still continue contributing to your 401(k) or IRAs if you are still employed, which can affect the whole discussion on RMDs and possible tax considerations. The SECURE Act 2.0 raised the RMD age to seventy-three from seventy-two. In addition, the latest legislation stipulates the RMD age will increase to seventy-five for those born in 1960 or later.[57]

If you don't need income from your retirement accounts, RMDs can seem like more of a tax burden than an income boon. While some people prefer to reinvest their RMDs, this comes with the possibility of additional taxation: You'll pay income taxes on your RMDs and then potential capital gains taxes on the growth of your investments. If you are legacy-minded, there are other ways to use RMDs, many of which have tax benefits.

### *SECURE 2.0 Act provisions*

In addition to changes imposed for RMD ages, Secure Act 2.0 also expanded access to retirement savings using different methods. Provisions in the legislation go into effect at different times, ranging from 2023-25.

---

[56] Jim Probasco. Investopedia. October 20, 2023. "SECURE 2.0 Act of 2022: Overview, Rules, Limits" https://www.investopedia.com/secure-2-0-definition-5225115

[57] Ibid.

- Beginning January 2, 2024, plan participants can access up to $1,000 (once a year) from retirement savings for emergency, personal, or family expenses without paying a 10 percent early-withdrawal penalty.
- Beginning January 2, 2024, employees can establish a Roth emergency savings account of up to $2,500 per participant.
- Beginning January 2, 2024, domestic abuse survivors can withdraw the lesser of $10,000 or 50 percent of their retirement account without penalty.[58]
- Beginning January 1, 2023, victims of a qualified, federally declared disaster can withdraw up to $22,000 from their retirement account without penalty.[59]

### *Permanent Life Insurance*

One way to turn those pesky RMDs into a legacy is through permanent life insurance. Assuming you need the death benefit coverage and can qualify for it medically, if properly structured, these products can pass on a sizeable death benefit to your beneficiaries — tax-free — as part of your general legacy plan.

### *ILIT*

Another way to use RMDs toward your legacy is to work with an estate planning attorney to create an irrevocable life insurance trust (ILIT). This is basically a permanent life insurance policy placed within a trust. Because the trust is irrevocable, you would relinquish control of it, but unlike with just a permanent life insurance policy, your death benefit won't count toward your taxable estate.

---

[58] Betterment editors. Betterment. February 24, 2023. "SECURE Act 2.0: Signed into Law" https://www.betterment.com/work/resources/secure-act-2

[59] Charlie Pastor. The Motley Fool. February 16, 2023. "Law Opens New Doors for Penalty-Free Retirement Account Distributions" www.fool.com/the-ascent/buying-stocks/articles/law-opens-new-doors-for-penalty-free-retirement-account-distributions

### *Annuities*

Because annuities can be tax-deferred, using all or a portion of your RMDs to fund an annuity contract can be one way to further delay taxation while guaranteeing your income payments (either to you or your loved ones) later. Of course, this assumes you don't need the RMD income during your retirement.

### *Qualified Charitable Distributions*

If you are charity-minded, you may use your RMDs toward a charitable organization instead of using them for income. You must do this directly from your retirement account (you can't take the RMD check and *then* pay the charity) for your withdrawals to be qualified charitable distributions (QCDs), but this is one way of realizing some of the benefits of a charitable legacy during your own lifetime. You will not need to pay taxes on your QCDs, and they won't count toward your annual charitable tax deduction limit; plus, you'll be able to see how the organization you are supporting uses your donations. You should consult a financial professional on how to correctly make a QCD.

## Roth IRAs

Since the Taxpayer Relief Act of 1997, there has been a different kind of retirement account — or "tax wrapper" — available to the public: the Roth. Roth IRAs and Roth 401(k)s each differ from their traditional counterparts in one big way: You pay your taxes on the front end. Once your post-tax money is in the Roth account, as long as you follow the rules and limitations of that account, your distributions are truly tax-free. You won't pay income tax when you take withdrawals, so in turn, you don't have to worry about RMDs. However, Roth accounts have the same limitations as traditional 401(k)s and IRAs when it comes to withdrawing money before age fifty-nine-and-one-half, with the added stipulation that the account must have been open for at least five years for the account holder to make withdrawals.

When doing a Roth conversion, we need to be on the lookout for how much room we have left in the tax bracket. Depending on how aggressive you want to be, we may purposefully jump a tax bracket or two. We also need to be aware if this will cause your Social Security to become taxable that year if it wasn't going to be already. It may still make sense to do so, but you need to at least be aware. Lastly, if you are age sixty-five or older and on Medicare, we will need to be cognizant of the impact of the conversion of Medicare premiums.

Medicare premiums go up at certain levels of MAGI (modified adjusted gross income). If it is just a small increase and the bigger-picture tax savings offset it, then it may still make sense to convert. If it is a substantial increase, then you may choose to toe the line and convert enough to get close, but not jump over the line.

There are a lot of moving parts here, and if it feels overwhelming, that's normal. The good news is that now, a capable financial planner that invests in the appropriate software and collaborates with your tax professional can help you figure these things out.

# Taking Charge

As mentioned earlier, the 401(k) and IRA have largely replaced pensions, but they aren't an equal trade.

Pensions are employer-funded; the money feeding into them is money that wouldn't ever show up on your pay stub. Because 401(k)s are self-funded, you must actively and consciously save. This distinction has made a difference when it comes to funding retirement. Fidelity Investments published a study detailing that the average 401(k) balance for a person aged fifty-five to sixty-four is $244,750, but the median likely tells the full story. The median 401(k) balance for a person aged fifty-five to sixty-four is $87,571. Those figures reflect Vanguard accounts from 2024.[60]

There can be many reasons why people underfund their retirement plans, like being overwhelmed by investment choices or taking withdrawals from IRAs when they leave an employer. Still, the reason at the top of the list seems to be this: People simply aren't participating to begin with.

So, whether you use a 401(k) with an employer or an IRA alternative with a private company separate from your workplace, the most important retirement savings decision you can make is to sock away your money somewhere in the first place.

---

[60] Arielle O'Shea. Elizabeth Ayoola. NerdWallet. June 26, 2024. "The Average 401(k) Balance by Age" https://www.nerdwallet.com/article/investing/the-average-401k-balance-by-age

CHAPTER 7

# Annuities

In my practice, I offer my clients a variety of products — from securities to insurance — designed to help them work toward their financial goals. You may be wondering: Why single out a single product in this book?

Well, while most of my clients have a pretty good understanding of business and finance, I sometimes find those who have the impression magic must be involved. Some people assume there is a magic finance wand we can wave to change years' worth of savings into a strategy for retirement income. But it's not as easy as a goose laying golden eggs or the Fairy Godmother turning a pumpkin into a coach!

Finances aren't magic; it takes lots of hard work and, typically, several financial products and strategies to pull together a complete retirement plan. Of all the financial products I work with, it seems people find none more mysterious than annuities. And, if I may say, even some of those who recognize the word "annuity" have a limited understanding of the product. So, in the interest of demystifying annuities, let me tell you a little about what an annuity is.

In general, insurance is a financial hedge against risk. Car owners buy auto insurance to protect their finances in case they injure someone or someone injures them. Homeowners have house insurance to protect their homes in case of a fire, flood, or another disaster. People have life insurance to help protect their finances in case of untimely death. Almost juxtaposed to life insurance, people have annuities in case of a long life; annuities can give you financial confidence by providing consistent and reliable income payments.

The basic premise of an annuity is that you, the annuitant, pay an insurance company some amount in exchange for their contractual guarantee they will pay you income for a certain time period. How that company pays you, for how long, and how much they offer are all determined by the annuity contract you enter into with the insurance company.

# The Ways You Get Paid

There are several ways an annuity contract can provide income: annuitization, income riders, partial surrenders, and settlement options for heirs.

## Annuitization

When someone "annuitizes" a contract, it is the point where they turn on the income stream. Once a contract has been annuitized, there is no going back. With annuities, if the policyholder lives longer than the insurance company planned, the insurance company is still obligated to pay them, even if the payments end up being way more than the contract's actual value.

If, however, the policyholder dies an untimely death, depending on the contract type, the insurance company may keep anything left of the money that funded the annuity. Nothing would be paid out to the contract holder's survivors. You see where that could make some people balk? Now, modern annuities rarely rely on annuitization for the income portion of the contract and instead have so many bells and whistles that the old concept of annuitization seems outdated. However, because this is still an option, it's important to at least understand the basic concept.

## Riders

Speaking of bells and whistles, let's talk about riders. Modern annuities have a lot of different options these days, many in the form of riders you can add to your contract for a fee.[61] The fee typically amounts to 0.1 percent to 1 percent of the contract value per year.[62] Each rider has its particulars, and the types of riders available will vary by the type of annuity contract purchased, but I'll just briefly outline some of these little extras:

- Lifetime income rider: Contract guarantees you an enhanced or flexible income for life
- Death benefit rider: Contract pays an enhanced death benefit to your beneficiaries, even if you have annuitized
- Return of premium rider: Guarantees you (or your beneficiaries) will at least receive back the premium value of the annuity
- Long-term care rider: Provides a certain amount, sometimes as much as twice the normal income benefit amount for a period of time to help pay for long-term care if the contract holder is moved to a nursing home or assisted living situation

This isn't an extensive look, and usually, the riders have fancier names based on the issuing company, like "Lorem Ipsum Insurance Company Income Preferred Bonus Fixed Index Annuity rider," but I just wanted to show you what some of the general options are in layperson's terms.

## Partial Surrender

Most annuities offer a free withdrawal provision that is often referred to as a partial surrender. An annuity contract typically

---

[61] Shawn Plummer. The Annuity Expert. 2024. "A Guide to Annuity Fees" https://www.annuityexpertadvice.com/types-of-annuities/annuity-fees/
[62] Shawn Plummer. The Annuity Expert. 2024. "Annuity Fees: What You Need To Know" https://www.annuityexpertadvice.com/types-of-annuities/annuity-fees/

allows for an annual withdrawal of up to 10 percent of the account value or of the premium originally paid. The option to make this withdrawal, typically without penalty, can be used as a tool to help with your income planning strategies. Keep in mind, the withdrawal is subject to income taxes and an additional 10 percent IRS penalty if you're under age fifty-nine-and-one-half.

This percentage can be accessed during the surrender period and can be a sound strategy, especially for a client who does not require a regular influx of income provided by a rider. After the surrender value period, the holder of the annuity can access the annuity without losing control of the account value.

I find the partial surrender strategy to often be effective for my clients, particularly if they do not need regular income generated through the use of a rider. A partial surrender allows for the annuity holder to just take out funds when a need arises.

## Settlement Options

While any value of an annuity left to beneficiaries upon the annuity holder's death is fairly self-explanatory, there is a point worth raising. Heirs have different settlement options they can consider, including opportunities for lump sums, periodic payments, or specific payouts.

Specific payouts are often based on tax considerations involving a beneficiary or multiple beneficiaries. As an advanced tax planning measure, I have clients who have addressed tax implications with their heirs regarding the most advantageous method for arranging a settlement option that eases any tax burden on the beneficiary.

# Types of Annuities

Annuities break down into four basic types: immediate, variable, fixed, and fixed index.

## Immediate

Immediate annuities primarily rely on annuitization to provide income. You give the insurance company a lump sum up front, and your payments begin immediately. Once you begin receiving income payments, the transaction is irreversible, and you can no longer access your money in a lump sum. When you die, any remaining contract value is typically forfeited to the insurance company.

All other annuity contract types are "deferred" contracts, meaning you fund your policy as a lump sum or over a period of years. You give it the opportunity to grow over time — sometimes years, sometimes decades.

## Variable

A variable annuity is an insurance contract as well as a security product. It's sold by insurance companies, but only through someone who is also registered to sell security products. With a variable annuity contract, the insurance company invests your premiums in sub-accounts that are tied to the stock market.

This makes it a bit different from the other annuity contract types because it is the only contract where your money is subject to losses because of market declines. Your contract value has a greater opportunity to grow, but it also stands to lose. Additionally, your contract's value will be subject to the underlying investment's fees and limitations, including management fees. Once it is time for you to receive income from the contract, the insurance company will pay you a certain income, locked in at whatever your contract's value was.*

* A variable annuity is sold by prospectus. Carefully read the prospectus before purchasing a variable annuity.

## Fixed

A traditional fixed annuity is pretty straightforward. You purchase a contract with a guaranteed interest rate, and when you are ready, the insurance company will make regular income payments to you at whatever payout rate your contract guarantees. Those payments will continue for the rest of your life and, if you choose, for the remainder of your spouse's life.

Fixed annuities don't typically offer significant upside potential, but many people like them for their guarantees and predictability. After all, if your Aunt May lives to be ninety-five, knowing she has a paycheck later in life can be her mental and financial safety net. Unlike variable annuities, which are subject to market risk and might be up one year and down the next, you can easily calculate the value of your fixed annuity over your lifetime.

## Fixed Index

To recap, variable annuities take on more risk to offer more possibilities to grow. Fixed annuities have less potential growth, but they protect your principal. In the last couple of decades, many insurance companies have retooled their product line to offer fixed indexed annuities, which are sort of midway between variable and fixed annuities on that risk/reward spectrum. Fixed index annuities offer greater growth potential than traditional fixed annuities but less than variable annuities. Like traditional fixed annuities, however, fixed index annuities are protected from downside market losses.

Fixed index annuities earn interest that is tied to an external market index, meaning that instead of your contract value growing at a set interest rate like a traditional fixed annuity, it has the potential to grow within a range. Your contract's value is credited interest based on the performance of an external market index like the S&P 500® while never being invested in the market itself. You can't invest in the S&P 500® directly, but based on when your contract credits interest to your account (e.g., one year – point-to-point, two years – point-to-point, etc.), your annuity has the potential to earn interest based on the chosen index's performance. The interest is subject to limits set by the company (such as caps, spreads, and participation rates).

For instance, if your contract caps your interest at 5 percent, then in a year that the S&P 500® gains 3 percent, your annuity value increases 3 percent. If the S&P 500® gains 35 percent, your annuity value gets a 5 percent interest bump. But since your money isn't actually invested in the market with a fixed index annuity, if the market nosedives (such as happened during 2000, 2008, 2020, and 2022, anyone?), you won't see any increase in your contract value. Insurance carriers charge Mortality & Expense fees (M&E fees) and may charge additional administrative fees to maintain the insurance policy contract that can lower your contract value. Conversely, there will also be no decrease in your contract value, no matter how badly the market performs. As long as you follow the terms of the contract, you won't lose any of the interest you were credited in previous years.

So, what if the S&P 500® shows a market loss of 30 percent? Your contract value isn't going anywhere unless you purchased an optional rider. This charge will still come out of your annuity value each year, along with M&E fees and possibly administrative fees). For those who are more interested in protection than significant growth potential, fixed index annuities can be an attractive option. When the stock market has a long period of positive performance, a fixed index annuity can enjoy conservative growth. And during stretches where the stock market is erratic and stock values across the board take significant losses? Fixed index annuities won't lose anything due to the stock market volatility.

Nowadays, it's pretty easy for a small group of people to trumpet information in the media or on social media, and it creates a narrative. The narrative may or may not be true, and it's usually created to reinforce the point that someone is trying to make.

In the financial world, this happens often. There are narratives that have been formed around different types of investments, with annuities being one of them. For some, it's another A word. Others absolutely love them. For me, I don't look at any financial instrument as something I like or don't like. Everything has its place.

## Other Things to Know About Annuities

We just explained the four kinds of annuity contracts available, but all of them have some commonalities as annuities.

For all annuities, the contractual guarantees are only as strong as the insurance company that sells the product, which makes it important to thoroughly check the credit ratings of any company whose products you are considering.

Annuities are tax-deferred, meaning you don't have to pay taxes on interest earnings each year as the contract value grows. Instead, you will pay ordinary income taxes on your withdrawals. These are meant to be long-term products, so like other tax-deferred or tax-advantaged products, if you begin taking withdrawals from your contract before age fifty-nine-and-one-half, you may also have to pay a 10 percent federal tax penalty. Also, while annuities are generally considered illiquid, some contracts allow you to withdraw up to 10 percent of your contract value every year. Withdraw any more, however, and you could incur additional surrender penalties.

Keep in mind, your withdrawals will deplete the accumulated cash value, death benefit, and possibly the rider values of your contract.

In times when interest rates are high, fixed index annuities can be an effective financial tool. For someone nearing or in retirement, this can also serve as a hedge against a sequence of returns risk. This can also be described as the chance that the bad years of the market happen early in your retirement instead of them happening towards the end of retirement. When you are taking withdrawals from a market-based account and there is another 2008-type downturn, you could be making those losses real instead of just a paper loss like you were used to when you were working. Having money in a guaranteed place like a fixed index annuity could provide a place to pull the money you need to live on that year from a place that didn't lose money in the market, and therefore help offset the sequence of returns risk.

Annuities aren't for everyone, but it's important to understand them before saying "yea" or "nay" on whether they fit into your plan; otherwise, you're not operating with complete information, wouldn't you agree? Regardless, you should talk to a financial professional who can help you understand annuities, dissect your particular financial needs, and show you whether an annuity is appropriate for your retirement income plan.

CHAPTER 8

# Estate and Legacy Planning Strategies

In my practice, I devote a significant portion of my time to matters of estate and legacy planning strategies. That doesn't mean drawing up wills or trusts or putting together powers of attorney or anything like that. After all, I'm not an estate planning attorney. But I am a financial professional, and what part of the "estate" isn't affected by money matters?

I've included this chapter because I have seen many people do estate planning wrong. Clients, or clients' families, have come in after experiencing a death in the family and have found themselves in the middle of probate, high taxes, or a discovery of something unforeseen (often long-term care) draining the estate.

I have also seen people do estate planning right: clients or families who visit my office to talk about legacies and ways to make them last, and adult children who have room to grieve without an added burden of unintended costs or stress from a family fractured because of inadequate planning.

I'll share some of these stories here. However, I'm not going to give you specific advice since everyone's situation is unique. I would advise you to speak with an estate planning attorney for specific advice. I only want to give you some things to think about and to underscore the importance of planning ahead.

Over the years, we have forged professional relationships with several attorneys. I believe that if you are getting something important done, such as an estate plan, you should hire an estate planning attorney who only does estate planning.

This might not be the time to call on the local general practitioner who is fighting traffic tickets and DUIs in the morning and then drafting a trust in the afternoon. Nothing against those folks, but you wouldn't go to the family doctor for heart surgery, either.

In addition, you want an attorney who is a good communicator because getting your estate plan funded is just as important as the document itself. Funding is the process of updating account titling and beneficiaries to align your assets with how the legal documents have been drafted. Often, a good attorney and a good financial advisor will work to remove as much of that task from your plate as possible.

Sometimes estate planning is just knowing what steps to take with the finances after one spouse dies. I recently had a client who I worked with for several years become terminally ill with cancer. One of the last things she did before she passed away was call me out to her house to help clean up the financial documents that she had accumulated over the years. More importantly, she wanted me to meet her husband, whom I had never met prior because he was never involved with the finances (I strongly encourage both spouses to attend retirement planning meetings for this exact reason, by the way).

It was important to her that he had someone to be there for him because she knew he would have a difficult time knowing what to do once she was gone. He was so grateful that he knew what the next steps were going to be because prior to that, he had no idea where the money was going to come from to pay the bills. It felt good knowing that I had helped remove a big burden from his mind. Just before I left, she gave me a hug and thanked me. I will never forget that feeling of knowing that was going to be the last memory and the last time I would ever see her.

## You Can't Take It With You

When it comes to legacy and estate planning strategies, the most important thing is to *do it.* I have heard people from clients to celebrities (rap artist Snoop Dogg comes to mind) say they aren't interested in what happens to their assets when they die because they'll be dead. That's certainly one way to look at it, but I think that's a very selfish way to go about things. We all have people and causes we care about, and those who care about us. Even if the people we love don't *need* what we leave behind, they can still be fined or legally tied up in the probate process or burial costs if we don't plan for those. And that's not even considering what happens if you become incapacitated at some point while you are still alive. Having a plan in place can greatly help reduce the stress of those responsibilities on your loved ones; it's just a loving thing to do.

# Documents

There are a few documents that lay the groundwork for legacy planning. You've probably heard of all or most of them, but I'd like to review what they are and how people commonly use them. These are all things you should talk about with an estate planning attorney to establish your legacy.

## Powers of Attorney

A power of attorney, or POA, is a document giving someone the authority to act on your behalf and in your best interests. These come in handy in situations where you cannot be present (think of a vacation where you get stuck in Canada), or for durable powers of attorney (DPOA), even when you are incapacitated (think in a coma or coping with dementia).

It is important to have powers of attorney in place and to appoint someone you trust to act on your behalf in these matters. Have you ever heard of someone who was incapacitated after a car accident, whether from head trauma or being in a coma for weeks — sometimes months? Do you think their bills stopped coming due during that time? I like my phone company and my bank, but neither one is about to put a moratorium on sending me bills — particularly not for an extended or interminable period. Someone with your power of attorney would have the authority to pay your mortgage or cancel your cable while you are unable.

***You can have multiple attorneys-in-fact and require them to act jointly.***

What this looks like: Do you think two heads are better than one? One man, Chris, significantly relied on his two sons' opinions for both his business and personal matters. He appointed both sons as attorneys-in-fact (AIFs), requiring both their signoffs for his medical and financial matters.

***You can have multiple attorneys-in-fact who can act independently.***

What this looks like: Irene had three children with whom she routinely stayed. They lived in different areas of the country, which she thought was an advantage; one month she might be hiking out West, the next she could enjoy the newest off-Broadway production, and the next she could soak up some Southern sun. She named her three children as independently authorized attorneys-in-fact, so if something happened, no matter where she was, the child closest could step in to act on her behalf.

***You can have attorneys-in-fact who have different responsibilities.***

What this looks like: Although Luke's friend Claire, a nurse, was his go-to and attorney-in-fact for health-related issues, financial matters usually made her nervous, so he appointed his good neighbor, Matt, as his attorney-in-fact in all of his financial and legal matters.

In addition to POAs, it may be helpful to have an advanced health care directive (HCD), which is sometimes referenced as a ***living will.*** This is a document where you have pre-decided what choices you would make about different health scenarios. An advanced health care directive can help ease the burden for your medical attorney-in-fact and loved ones, particularly when it comes to end-of-life care.

You may remember the famous Terri Schiavo case in Florida where the wife was being kept alive artificially. The husband wanted to end life support, and the parents wanted to keep her going. This became a big contested court battle because there was no medical POA in place to give explicit authority to anyone to make the decision, nor were there any directives for anyone to know what her wishes were.[63]

## Wills

Perhaps the most basic document of legacy planning, a will is a legal document wherein you outline your wishes for your estate. When it comes to your estate after your death, having a will is the foundation of your legacy. Without one, your loved ones are left behind to guess what you would have wanted, and the court will likely split your assets according to the state's probate laws. As far as anyone knows, maybe that's exactly what you wanted, right? Because even if you told your nephew he could have your car he's been driving, if it's not in writing, it still might go to the brother, sister, son, or daughter to whom you aren't speaking.

However, it may not be enough just to have a will. Even with a will, your assets will be subject to probate. Probate is what we call the state's process for determining a will's validity. A judge will go through your will to question if it conflicts with state law, if it is the most up-to-date document, if you were mentally competent at the time it was in order, etc. For some, this is a

---

[63] Ashley Sadler. Oregon Right to Life. April 1, 2024. "March 31 Marked the 19th Anniversary of Terri Schiavo's Death" https://www.ortl.org/2024/04/march-31-marks-19th-anniversary-of-terri-schiavo-death/

quick, easily resolved process. For others, particularly if someone steps forward to contest the will, it may take years to settle, all the while subjecting the assets to court costs and attorney's fees.

Another undesirable piece of the probate process is that it is a public process. That means anyone can go to the courthouse, ask for copies of the case, and discover your assets. They can also see who is slated to receive what and who is disputing.

The famous singer Aretha Franklin, also known as the Queen of Soul, surprisingly passed away without estate planning documents in place. The estate was worth millions of dollars. She died in 2018, resulting in a lengthy squabble over her estate. Not only did her heirs not gain their inheritance quickly, but the costs escalated for attorney fees.[64]

I'm sure it's a stressful time for everyone involved. In addition, this is a public process since it's going through probate. This is all happening about an hour away from my house, so I could actually drive over there and get information on what is happening if I wanted. Had she only had a few estate planning documents in place, this headache could have been avoided.

It's also important to remember beneficiary designations trump wills. So, that large life insurance policy? What if, when you bought it fifteen years ago, you wrote your ex-husband's name on the beneficiary line? Even if you stipulate otherwise in your will, the company that holds your policy will pay out to your ex-spouse. Or how about the thousands of dollars in your IRA you dedicated to the children thirty years ago, but one of your children was killed in a car accident, leaving his wife and two toddlers behind? That IRA is going to transfer to your remaining children, with nothing for your daughter-in-law and grandchildren.

---

[64] Kenneth C. Russell. Russell Law. March 14, 2024. "Lessons from Aretha Frank;in's Estate Woes" https://russell.legal/blog/lessons-from-aretha-franklins-estate-woes/

That may paint a grim portrait, but I can't underscore enough the importance of working with a skilled estate planning attorney to keep your will and beneficiary designations up to date as your life changes.

## Trusts

Another piece of legacy planning to consider are trusts. A trust is set up through an attorney who appoints and authorizes a trusted party or trustee(s) to administer the trust (e.g., make decisions, manage the assets in the trust, distribute funds from the trust, etc.) according to the provisions of the trust agreement.

Many people are skeptical of trusts because they assume they are only appropriate for the fabulously wealthy. A simple trust will likely cost more than $1,000 if prepared by an estate planning attorney, and fees can be higher for couples.[65] However, a trust can help you avoid both the expense and publicity of probate, provide a more immediate transfer of wealth, avoid some taxes, and provide you greater control over your legacy.

For instance, if you want to set aside some funds for a grandchild's college education, you can make it a requirement that they enroll in classes before your trust will dispense any funds. Like a will, beneficiary designations will override your trust conditions, so you still should be keeping your beneficiary designations on insurance policies, investment accounts (e.g., 401(k)s, IRAs, etc.), and other assets up to date.

Like any financial or legal consideration, there are many options these days beyond the simple "yes or no" question of whether to have a trust. For one thing, you will need to consider whether you want your trust to be revocable (you can change

---

[65] Rickie Houston. SmartAsset. April 5, 2023. "How Much Does It Cost to Set Up a Trust? https://smartasset.com/estate-planning/how-much-does-it-cost-to-set-up-a-trust

the terms while you are alive) or irrevocable (can't be changed; you are no longer the "owner" of the contents).

A brief note here about irrevocable trusts: Although they have significant and greater tax benefits, they are still subject to a Medicaid look-back period. If you transfer your assets into an irrevocable trust in an attempt to shelter them from a Medicaid spend-down, you will be ineligible for Medicaid coverage of long-term care for five years. However, an irrevocable trust can avoid both probate and estate taxes, and it can even help protect assets from legal judgments against you.

Another thing to remember when it comes to trusts, in general, is that even if you have set up a trust, you must remember to fund it. In my seventeen years of work, I've had numerous clients come to me assuming they have helped protect their assets with a trust. When we talk about taxes and other pieces of their legacy, it turns out they never retitled any assets or changed any paperwork on the assets they wanted in the trust. So, please remember, a trust is just a bunch of fancy legal papers if you haven't followed through on retitling your assets.

## Taxes

Although charitable contributions, trusts, and other tax-efficient strategies can reduce your tax bill, it's unlikely your estate will be passed on entirely tax-free. Yet, when it comes to building a legacy that can last for generations, taxes can be one of the heaviest drains on the impact of your hard work.

For 2024, the federal estate exemption was $13.61 million per individual and $27.22 million for a married couple, with estates facing up to a 40 percent tax rate after that.[66] Currently, the new estate limits are set to increase with inflation until

---

[66] Katelyn Washington. Kiplinger. April 24, 2024. "What's the 2024 Estate Tax Exemption?" https://www.kiplinger.com/taxes/estate-tax-exemption-amount-increases

January 1, 2026, when they will "sunset" back to the inflation-adjusted 2017 limits.[67] And that's not taking into account the various state regulations and taxes regarding estate and inheritance transfers.

Another tax concern "frequent flyer": retirement accounts.

Your IRA or 401(k) can be a source of tax issues when you pass away. For one thing, taking funds from a sizeable account can trigger a large tax bill. However, if you leave the assets in the account, there are still required minimum distributions (RMDs), which will take effect even after you die. If you pass the account to your spouse, they can keep taking your RMDs as is, or your spouse can retitle the account in their name and receive RMDs based on their life expectancy. Remember, if you don't take your RMDs, the IRS will take up to 25 percent of your required distribution (10 percent if corrections are made in a timely fashion). You will still have to pay income taxes whenever you withdraw that money. Provisions in the original SECURE Act require anyone who inherits your IRA, with few exceptions (your spouse, a beneficiary less than ten years younger, or a disabled adult child, to name a few), to empty the account within ten years of your death.

Also — and this is a pretty big also — check with an estate planning attorney if you are considering putting your IRA or 401(k) in a trust. An improperly titled beneficiary form for the IRA could mean a difference of thousands of dollars in taxes. This is just one more reason to work with a financial professional who can strategically partner with an estate planning attorney and a tax advisor to diligently check your decisions.

---

[67] Josie M. Metzler. Adam Campbell. Husch Blackwell. June 13, 2024. "Understanding the 2026 Changes to the Estate, Gift, and Generation-Skipping Tax Exemptions" https://www.huschblackwell.com/newsandinsights/understanding-the-2026-changes-to-the-estate-gift-and-generation-skipping-tax-exemptions

CHAPTER 9

# Women Retire Too

I help men, women, and families from all walks of life on their journey to and through retirement. However, we want to address the female demographic specifically. Why? To be perfectly blunt, women are more likely to deal with poverty than men when they reach retirement.

The overall poverty rate for women slightly exceeds the rate for men, but among those sixty-five years and older, 11.2 percent of women live at the poverty rate compared to 9 percent of men.[68]

The topics, products, and strategies I cover elsewhere in this book are meant to help address retirement concerns for men *and* women. Still, the dire statistic above is a reminder that much of traditional planning is geared toward men: male careers, male lifespans, and male health care. The bottom line is women's career paths often look much different than men's, so why would their retirement planning look the same?

Women often embrace different roles and values than men as workers, wives, mothers, and daughters. They are more apt to take on roles as caretakers; thus, women are likely to spend portions of their lives making hard shifts between family and careers. Time out of the workforce means less income

---

[68] Administration for Community Living. May 2024. "2023 Profile of Older Americans" https://acl.gov/sites/default/files/Profile%20of%20OA/ACL_ProfileOlderAmericans2023_508.pdf

accumulation for investments and retirement. Also, non-working years count as zeroes when calculating Social Security benefits. Women who strongly value family and community tend to focus on lifetime gifting and legacy funding, sometimes to the detriment of their own lifestyles.

These unique choices, challenges, and hurdles make a solid case that women deserve special consideration from financial professionals. This argument is further promoted by the fact that 68 percent of men in the U.S. age sixty-five and older happen to be married, compared to 47 percent of women in that age classification.[69] Single women don't have the opportunity to capitalize on the resource pooling and potential economies of scale accompanying a marriage or partnership.

I have experienced that single, widowed, and divorced women still appreciate having that second person to bounce their financial decisions off of. And being unmarried, they only have one Social Security income to live on, so the pressure is greater. Oh, and there is the unfair disadvantage of paying higher income taxes. I have experienced that married women sometimes might have let their husbands take the lead on financial matters. However, they put a lot of value in being a part of the retirement planning meetings so they at least have a sense of what is going on. Should something happen to him, they know that they have someone who will be there for them.

## Be Informed

With all the couples I've seen, there is almost always an "alpha" when it comes to finances. It isn't always men. For many of my coupled clients, the wife is the alpha who keeps the books and budgets and knows where all of the family's assets are, down to the penny. Yet, statistically, among baby boomers, it is usually a man who runs the books. However, as time goes on, it looks

---

69 Ibid.

like the ratio of male to female financial alphas is evening out, based on my experience speaking with couples.

Because most of the baby boomer alphas are men, there is an all too familiar scene in many financial offices across the country: A woman comes into an appointment carrying a sack full of unopened envelopes. Often through tears, she sits across the desk from a financial professional and apologizes her way through a conversation about what financial products she owns and where her income is coming from. She is recently widowed and was sure her spouse was taking care of the finances, but now she doesn't know where all their assets are kept, and her confidence in her financial outlook has wavered after walking through funeral expenses and realizing she's down to one income.

Often, she may be financially "okay." Yet, the uncertainty can be wearying, particularly when the family is already reeling from a loss. While this scenario sometimes plays out with men, in my experience, it's more likely to be a woman in that chair across from my desk. Although the practice has been leveling more and more in recent decades, for centuries, Western traditions have held money management down as being "a guy thing." But it doesn't have to be this way. This all-too-common scenario can be wiped away with just a little preparation.

## Talk to Your Spouse/ Work with a Financial Professional

While there are many factors affecting women's financial preparation for and situation in retirement, I cannot emphasize enough that the decision to be informed, to be a part of the conversation, and to be aware of what is going on with your finances is absolutely paramount to a confident retirement.

The breakdown regarding couples and finances seems to happen because of a lack of communication. The breakdown often seems to stem from no one other than the financial alpha knowing how much the family has and where. In the end, it doesn't matter who handles the money; it's about all parties being informed of what's going on financially.

There are a lot of ways to open the conversation about money. One woman, Ann, started a conversation with her husband, the financial alpha, by sitting down and saying, "Teach me how to be a widow." Perhaps that sounds grim, but it was to the point, and it spurred what she said was a very fruitful conversation. Couples sometimes have their first real conversation about money, assets, and their retirement income approach in our office. The important thing about having these conversations isn't where — it's *when*. The best "when" is as soon as possible.

Ann told me that after they got the conversation rolling, she and her husband spent a day — just one part of an otherwise dull weekend — going through everything she might need to know. They spent the better part of two decades together after that. When he died and she was widowed, she said the "widowhood" talk had made a huge difference. She knew who to call to talk through their retirement plan and where to call for the insurance policy.

She said the benefit of the weekend exercise they engaged in some twenty years earlier couldn't have been more apparent than when she ultimately accompanied a recently widowed friend to a financial appointment. Her friend was emotional the whole time, afraid she would run out of money any day. The financial professional ultimately showed the friend that she was financially in good shape, but not before the friend had already spent months worried that each check would exhaust her bank account. That's no way to live after losing a loved one. It was preventable had her deceased spouse and financial professional included her in a conversation about "widowhood."

## Spouse-Specific Options

One area where it might be especially important for spouses to be on the same page is when it comes to financial products or services with spousal options. A few that come to mind are pensions and Social Security, although life insurance and annuity policies can also potentially affect both spouses.

With pensions, taking the worker's life-only option is somewhat attractive. After all, the monthly payment is bigger. However, you and your spouse should discuss your options. When we're talking about both of you as opposed to just one lifespan, there is an increased likelihood that at least one of you will live a long, long time. This means the monthly payout will be less, but it also helps ensure that no matter which spouse outlives the other, no one will have to suffer the loss of a needed pension paycheck in their later retirement years.

While we covered Social Security options in a different chapter, I think some of the spousal information bears repeating. Particularly, if you worked exclusively inside the home for a significant number of years, you may want to talk about taking your Social Security benefits based on your spouse's work history. After all, Social Security is based on your thirty-five highest-earning years.

Things to remember about the spousal benefits:[70]

- Your benefit will be calculated as a percentage (up to 50 percent) of your spouse's earned monthly benefit at their full retirement age (or FRA).
- For you to begin receiving a spousal benefit, your spouse must have already filed for their benefits, and you must be at least sixty-two.
- You can qualify for a full half of your spouse's benefits if you wait until you reach FRA to file.
- Beginning your benefits earlier than your FRA will reduce your monthly check, but waiting to file until after FRA will not increase your benefits.

For divorcees:[71]

---

[70] Social Security Administration. 2024. "Family benefits" https://www.ssa.gov/family

[71] Social Security Administration. 2024. "Who can get Family benefits" https://www.ssa.gov/family/eligibility

- You may qualify for an ex-spousal benefit if ...
    a. You were married for a decade or more
    b. ***and*** you are at least sixty-two
    c. ***and*** you have been divorced for at least two years
    d. ***and*** you are currently unmarried
    e. ***and*** your ex-spouse is sixty-two (qualifies to begin taking Social Security)
- Your ex-spouse does not need to have filed for you to file on their benefit.
- Similar to spousal benefits, you can qualify for up to half of your ex-spouse's benefits if you wait to file until your FRA.
- If your ex-spouse dies, you may file to receive a widow/widower benefit on their Social Security record as long as you are at least age sixty and fulfill all the other requirements on the preceding alphabetized list.
    a. This will not affect the benefits of your ex-spouse's current spouse

For widow's (or widower's, for that matter) benefits:[72]

- You may qualify to receive as much as your deceased spouse would have received if ...
    a. You were married for at least nine months before their death
    b. ***or*** you would qualify for a divorced spousal benefit (if you were divorced and your ex-spouse dies)
    c. ***and*** you are at least sixty
    d. ***and*** you did not/have not remarried before age sixty
- You may earn delayed credits on your spouse's benefit *if* your spouse hadn't already filed for benefits when they died.

---

[72] Social Security Administration. 2024. "Survivor benefits" https://www.ssa.gov/survivor

- Other rules may apply to you if you are disabled or are caring for a deceased spouse's dependent or disabled child.

## Longevity

On average, women live longer than men. Most stats put average female longevity at about two years more than men. But averages are tricky things. In 2024, the eight oldest people in the world are all women. They range in age from 114 to 116 and include two Americans.[73]

It's an exciting time to be a woman, as their potential life paths are vast and less subject to judgment than probably at any point in history. Want to stay at home and raise children? Wonderful! Get a PhD in Astrophysics and work for NASA? Fantastic! Do a combination of both? It's happening! On one hand, women all have unique personalities, goals, ambitions, and passions. However, they share biological and instinctual traits that generally give rise to longer lives. On that note, the trend for women to live longer presents longstanding financial ramifications.

I have heard jokes from the guys that it is the women who drive the men crazy, and this is the reason men don't live as long. This is often followed by, "Well, if men didn't do so many stupid things, maybe they would live longer." Frankly, it's pretty enjoyable to witness the banter between a married couple sometimes. The point is, the difference in longevity is a reality that needs to be considered when planning retirement.

---

[73] Gerontology Wiki. 2024. "Oldest living people" https://gerontology.fandom.com/wiki/Oldest_living_people

## Simply Needing More Money in Retirement

Living longer in retirement means needing more money. Period. Barring a huge lottery win or some crazy stock market action, the date you retire is likely the point at which you have the most money you will ever have. Not to put too grim a spin on it, but the problem with longevity is the further you get away from that date, the further your dollars have to stretch. If you only planned to live to a nice eighty-something but instead live to a nice 100-something, that is *two decades* you will need to account for monetarily.

To put this in perspective, let's say you like to drink coffee as an everyday splurge. Not accounting for inflation or leap years, a $4 cup-a-day habit is $29,200 over a two-decade span. Now, think of all the things you like to do that cost money. Add those up for twenty years of unanticipated costs. I think you'll see what I mean.

## More Health Care Needs

In addition to the cost of living for a longer lifespan is the fact that aging — plain and simple — means more health care, and more health care means more money. Women are survivors. They suffer from the morbidity-mortality paradox, which states women suffer more non-fatal illnesses throughout their lifetime than men, who experience fewer illnesses but higher mortality.

Women have been found to seek treatment more often when not feeling well and emphasize staying healthy when older, according to studies. Survival, I believe, is on the side of the woman. However, surviving things (such as cancer) also means more checkups later in life.

A statistical concern for women involves the prospect of long-term care. Long-term care for women lasts 3.7 years on average compared to 2.2 years for men.[74]

## Widowhood

Not only do women typically live longer than their same-age male counterparts, but they also stand a greater chance of living alone as they age. Some divorce, separate, or never marry. Among those age sixty-five and over, 35 percent of women live alone compared to 22.5 percent of men.[75]

I don't write this to scare people; rather, I think it's fundamentally important to prepare my female clients for something that may be a startling *but very likely* scenario. At some point, most women will have to handle their financial situations on their own. A little preparation can go a long way, and having a basic understanding of your household finances and the "who, what, where, and how much" of your family's assets is incredibly useful. It can prevent a tragic situation from being more traumatic.

In my opinion, the financial services industry sometimes underserves women in these situations. Some financial professionals tend to alienate women, even when their spouses are alive. I've heard several stories of women who sat through meeting after meeting without their financial professional ever addressing a single question to them.

In our firm, when working with couples, we work hard to ensure our retirement income strategies work for *both* people. No matter who the financial alpha is, it's important for everyone affected by a retirement strategy to understand it.

---

[74] Lindsay Modglin. SingleCare. January 24, 2024. "Long-term care statistics 2024" https://www.singlecare.com/blog/news/long-term-care-statistics/

[75] United States Census Bureau. May 30, 2024. "Living Arrangements Varied Across Age Groups" https://www.census.gov/library/stories/2024/05/living-arrangements.html

### *Taxes*

One of the often-unexpected aspects of widowhood is the tax bill. Many women continue similar lifestyles to the ones they shared with their spouses. This, in turn, means continuing to have a similar need for income. However, after the death of a spouse, their taxes will be calculated based on a single filer's income table, which is much less forgiving than the couple's tax rates. With proper planning, your financial professional and tax advisor may be able to help you take the sting out of your new tax status.

## Caregiving

In addition to the financial burden created by caregiving responsibilities, many women often devote many hours each day to duties such as housekeeping and looking after loved ones. So then, when can women find the time to focus long and hard on financial matters?

Unfortunately, the impact and hardships created by traditional roles for women typically do not account for Social Security benefit losses or the losses of health care benefits and retirement savings. This also doesn't account for maternity care, mothers who homeschool, or women who leave the workforce to care for their children in any way.

I don't repeat these statistics to scare you. In America, about 53 million serve as unpaid caregivers,[76] and they spend roughly $7,000 annually on out-of-pocket caregiving costs.[77] Yet, I don't think you can quantify the *emotional* value of the care many women provide their elderly relatives or neighbors. So, to be clear, this shouldn't be taken as a "why not to provide

---

[76] Guardian. 2024. "Standing Up and Stepping In" https://connect.guardiangroupbenefits.com/l/503851/2023-12-15/6yw1b6/503851/1702675399bBkGiG78/Guardian_12th_Annual_WBS_Standing_Up_and_Stepping_In_1215.pdf

[77] Ella Vincent. Kiplinger. August 3, 2023. "The High Costs of Senior Caregiving" https://www.kiplinger.com/personal-finance/the-high-costs-of-senior-caregiving

caregiving" spiel. Instead, it should be seen as a call for "why to *prepare* for caregiving" or "how to lessen the financial and emotional burden of caregiving."

## Funding Your Own Retirement

For these reasons, women should be prepared to fund more of their own retirements. There are several savings options and products, including the spousal IRA. They are like a typical IRA except used by a person who's married. The working spouse must earn at least as much money as is contributed into the IRA.[78] This is something to consider, particularly for families where one spouse has dropped out of the workforce to care for a relative. Also, if you find yourself in a caregiving role, talk to your employer's human resources department. Some companies have paid leave, special circumstances, or sick leave options you could qualify for, making it easier to cope and helping you stay longer in the workforce.

## Saving Money

Women likely need more money to fund their retirements. But this doesn't have to be a significant burden. Women are often better at saving while taking less risk in their portfolios. One source identified many ways in which women are crushing this retirement component.[79]

- In a 2021 analysis of five million Fidelity customers over a ten-year period, women's investment rates of return outperformed men by .04 percent.

---

[78] Andrea Coombes. NerdWallet. July 26, 2024. "Spousal IRA: What It Is, How to Open One" https://www.nerdwallet.com/article/investing/spousal-ira-what-it-is-and-why-you-should-open-one

[79] Lyle Daly. The Motley Fool. February 20, 2024. "Investing for Women: What You Should Know" https://www.fool.com/research/women-in-investing-research/

- Wells Fargo found that women take approximately 82 percent of the risk men take.
- Meghan Railey, co-founder and CEO of Optas Capital, wrote, "While we have found that male clients tend to eagerly invest in the latest asset class everyone is talking about, like cryptocurrency, female clients do not generally jump on the shiny bandwagon."
- Women do a better job buying and holding quality stocks and avoid impulsive decisions. Staying invested for the long haul is often cited as the most effective investing strategy.
- Women remain calm and are less likely to liquidate their retirement accounts during market volatility.
- Lastly, Vanguard found women are less active investors, logging on to their accounts half as often as men and trading 40 percent less frequently.

With all the hurdles to retirement that are unique to women, it's exciting they inherently have an advantage when it comes to saving. This gives me reason to believe that as women get more involved in their finances, their families will continue to become more confident about retirement.

CHAPTER 10

# Charity

Wills and testaments, trusts, and powers of attorney are all pieces of what we often call legacy planning. But I would be remiss if I didn't address a piece of legacy preparation near and dear to my heart: charitable contributions.

Charity is one of those universal concepts that unites us as human beings. Consider football players who dedicate their resources to building homes for single moms, communities who help neighbors rebuild after catastrophes, groundskeepers who donate millions from under a mattress to their favorite university, or private donors who put impoverished children through school. These are the stories that inspire us and drive us to be better people.

There are many, many ways to pass money to your favorite charity, university, foundation, or public resource. Some include using qualified charitable distributions with mandatory withdrawals from your IRA; others lend themselves to establishing trusts. Whatever your preferred method of charitable distribution, the right financial professional will partner with a qualified tax advisor or estate planning attorney (or both) to discover how to help you make your contributions in a way that fits well within your own strategy for taxes. They help ensure your contributions are passed efficiently to your intended beneficiary.

# Where to Start?

We've all heard it is better to give than to receive, and science backs this up. Multiple studies show those who give to charity or volunteer experience less depression, lower blood pressure, higher self-esteem, and greater happiness.[80]

However, it's a common perception that retirees are less inclined to be charitable. It seems like reasoned logic — they're living on fixed incomes, and it's difficult to work charitable giving into conservative strategies designed to protect assets. But this counters the facts. In a recent study, more baby boomers donated to charities than any other generation. On average, the average gift per baby boomer is $1,212.[81]

So, how do we keep up or even increase our retirement donations? Well, as with all the other topics we cover in this book, step one is to build charitable giving into our retirement plans. Advanced planning can help you be sure your donations — at least in the monetary sense — are given in the most tax-efficient and effective way, both for you and the charity to which you contribute.

# Planned Giving: Lifetime

When we're talking about charitable contributions, it's important to distinguish between lifetime giving and charitable giving as part of a well-prepared estate plan.

The American tax system has many provisions to encourage charitable giving. I'm sure the reasoning goes something along the lines of, "If we, the people, were naturally able to care for

---

[80] Jeanne Segal. Lawrence Robinson. HelpGuide.org. August 21, 2024. "Volunteering and its Surprising Benefits" https://www.helpguide.org/articles/healthy-living/volunteering-and-its-surprising-benefits.htm

[81] Bill Allen. PayBee. May 24, 2024. "Fundraising Audience: Generations, Who Gives the Most and Why" https://w.paybee.io/post/fundraising-audience-generations-who-gives-the-most-and-why

the poor and vulnerable in our own communities through our own means, we collectively would need to pay fewer taxes to support federal aid to those same people." It's a wonderful consideration and one we should all aspire to. However, it becomes more difficult in practice as tax codes change and shift according to political administrations and other public considerations. Ensuring your charitable contributions are tax-efficient is not a one-time move — it requires yearly analysis.

It's important to remember your charitable giving is most effective when the combined amount of your *itemized* deductions is more than your *standard* deduction. Now, it isn't only charity that counts toward your itemized deductions. There are also medical expenses, mortgage interest, and other taxes such as real estate and state income taxes. Deductions change year-to-year, of course, but the IRS usually publishes the following year's charts in November. When you're itemizing deductions, you may typically deduct up to 60 percent of your adjusted gross (pre-tax) income, though in some cases, other limitations apply.[82]

Another thing to keep in mind if you are considering the tax implications of a charitable donation is that you must have a receipt, a canceled check, or some demonstrable way of recording the transaction. Specifically, if you are audited, you will need a donation acknowledgment receipt from the charity for any cash or non-cash amounts over $250. Additionally, many charitable activities aren't eligible for a tax deduction. Raffle tickets, charity event entrance fees, and those sorts of things are not typically counted as charitable deductions on your taxes. A quick rule of thumb is if you received something in return for your donation, it's not tax-deductible.

However, perhaps one of the most crucial things to keep in mind when it comes to the tax implications of charitable giving is "nonprofit" doesn't mean "tax-advantaged." The IRS keeps a

---

[82] Internal Revenue Service. August 20, 2024. "Charitable contribution deductions" https://www.irs.gov/charities-non-profits/charitable-organizations/charitable-contribution-deductions

long list of organizations that qualify for tax-deducted gifting in the Internal Revenue Code section 501(c)(3). Yet many excellent nonprofits and civic organizations are not 501(c)(3)s. That doesn't mean you shouldn't give to them. Truly, charity is *not* about tax deductions when it comes right down to it. It just means you shouldn't plan to include it as part of your tax-efficiency strategies.

Again, I would be remiss not to emphasize that these laws and definitions change year to year, so it is important to work with a team of qualified financial and tax professionals who can help you plan for the future and adjust to the times, in addition to verifying whether the charity you are considering is tax-exempt.

While impermanence seems to be a fixture of our tax system, one important aspect of charity tax law was made permanent for the foreseeable future. In 2015, Congress passed a budget deal signed into law by President Barack Obama. Among the provisions of the "Protecting Americans From Tax Hikes Act of 2015," which included this important measure:

> IRA charitable rollovers — at age seventy-and-one-half, owners of traditional IRAs can give up to $100,000 a year to a qualified charity directly from the IRA.[83] This is known as a qualified charitable distribution (QCD).

What makes this deduction so important is a person who uses an IRA to contribute to charity in this way can:

- Be charitable.
- Avoid having their RMDs push them into a higher tax bracket by instead gifting them to those in need.
- Take advantage of the tax-free aspect of a QCD when planning charitable gifting.
- Potentially use the tax break to offset other tax consequences, like the tax on appreciated assets or capital gains.

---

[83] Council on Foundations. 2024. "IRA Charitable Rollover" https://www.cof.org/content/ira-charitable-rollover-0#

With an allowance for IRA contributions after an individual reaches age seventy-three, QCDs will be adversely affected if a contribution is made to that IRA in the same year a QCD is withdrawn.

On another note, Medicare premiums are affected by your income. If you hit certain levels, your premiums go up. This is based on your Modified Adjusted Gross Income, sometimes known as MAGI (she sounds nice, doesn't she?).

An additional benefit of using QCD is that income doesn't get added to your MAGI. Whereas if you pulled it out of your IRA, put it in your bank account, and then donated it, it would count in the MAGI calculation. So basically, we often use QCDs and DAFs to offset the tax on IRAs to keep the IRS away. Now that is some alphabet soup! LOL.

## Planned Giving: After My Lifetime

For many charities, endowments and legacy gifts are the lifeblood that keeps them going. And for many of us, a large final gift is an excellent way to continue a legacy of giving into perpetuity. The financial reasons for final charitable gifts are many and (mostly) tax-based, much like the annual contributions we often give. A large final gift can be a good way to offload highly appreciated assets, allowing our favorite charities to experience the full use of an asset without us having to pay out a sizable tax bill.

Many charities have gone to great lengths to make this an attractive option, with some having preferences for certain donation types and strategies. For instance, many public entities, such as libraries and schools, have foundations to collect most of the donations and do major fundraising. Churches and universities often have special projects and intentional funding that stems from sizable endowments.

There are many financial vehicles to help you meet your charitable goals and give you benefits during your lifetime as well — from permanent life insurance policies to charitable trusts and annuities. That's why it's important to plan ahead and work with a goal in mind. If you have some idea of what end you want to achieve, it can be easier to find the estate attorneys, tax professionals, and financial professionals who will be best qualified to help.

## Non-Monetary Charitable Contributions

Ultimately, aside from tax breaks, good feelings, and the name on a park bench you might receive, your charitable contributions aren't about what you "get" in return. This is one other reason we should plan ahead for our good works; it's about doing the right thing.

Volunteering is one great, non-monetary way to support the charities and causes we believe in. As I noted earlier, research shows retirees who are active and engaged volunteers in their communities often have a better sense of purpose and report more happiness than those who aren't. In volunteering, we have a reason to get up in the morning, and we meet new people and make friends. These are all things that may previously have stemmed from your nine-to-five workday but tend to fall by the wayside after leaving the workforce, making this consideration even more important.

I have seen the gifting of time, not just treasures, be quite gratifying. There was this couple that I worked with, and at first, retirement was a bore for them. Their kids and grandkids lived far away. Their friends were their work friends. They just did not have many hobbies other than watching the Lions lose on Sundays, like myself.

Then they started getting active in the community, and they found a new purpose in volunteerism. They rediscovered what they did not even know they were missing in having built-in socialization time. The enjoyment of collaborating on projects and putting their talents to good use brought a deep sense of joy to them.

Our families are one way we leave a legacy. But charitable giving — with our time, our talents, and our treasure — allows us to extend our legacies even further, beyond passing on Grandpa's nose or Grandma's ticklish feet.

CHAPTER 11

# Finding a Financial Professional

If you count my paper route, I've been working since I was twelve years old. I worked through high school while playing three sports and through college to minimize the amount of student loans I would have (I wish I would have known that twenty years later, the government would just start magically making student loans disappear).

I held a wide variety of positions. I stocked shelves and bagged groceries at the grocery store where my mom worked. I was a gas station attendant. I threw two-by-fours around at a lumber yard for a summer. I drove a forklift at a pickle factory. I worked in the sporting goods department at Meijer. I was a shift manager of a Little Caesars, and I even delivered pizzas in the Upper Peninsula winters.

I'm not sure where the maturity came from at the time, but I remember telling myself that I wanted to work at several places. By doing so, I could learn what I liked and what I didn't about each job. I learned something at every stop, and I am grateful for that. In fact, I knew college was in my future after coming home sore every day from loading trucks with lumber by hand.

I remember sitting in class during my senior year of business school and thinking about what I really wanted to do for a career. It was tough on me not knowing what I was going to do when others seemed to know what was coming next. The great thing about a business degree is it is broad-based, and the bad thing about the degree is that it is broad-based. There is no obvious path forward from college like there is with a nursing or education degree.

So, I reflected on all of the job experiences I had by that point in my life. I realized that the times when I wasn't watching the clock and felt energized were when I was directly interacting with people. Meeting new people, helping them find what they need, getting to know them, and making them happy by solving their problems was rewarding.

Then I thought about what classes I enjoyed in college. Economics was by far my favorite. In my first economics class, the professor gave out the final exam on the first day of class and then again on the last day. That was his way of measuring to see what people learned during class (such an economist thing to do, by the way). I ended up acing the exam on day one. I was quite proud and slightly surprised that it just came so naturally to me. The science of how money and the economy worked seemed so logical. When I pulled out the things I liked about my jobs and combined them with the subject matter I enjoyed studying the most, voila! I knew I was destined to be a financial advisor!

The financial advisor industry is unique. The licensing and certifications you need to be in "the business" were not what I expected. It doesn't take years of schooling to enter the profession as a doctor or attorney might endure. However, there's a difference between someone just entering the industry to make money and those dedicated to receiving the licenses and experience necessary to help retirees truly take steps toward their financial goals.

What should you be looking for? For starters, find out what licenses the financial professional has. I recommend that they have their securities license in addition to their life insurance license. Securities mean they are allowed to advise on and recommend market-based investments like stocks, bonds, mutual funds, exchange-traded funds, etc. This could mean they have a Series 6, Series 7, or Series 65 license. Even if you aren't in the market for that type of investment, you want to work with a professional well-versed in all the investment options, not just the ones that life insurance alone will allow them to sell. If multiple advisors work for that firm, do they all have multiple licenses or just a couple? What licenses does the owner or founder have? That might be an indicator of the culture of the firm.

In my opinion, licensing is just the beginning question. It's possible to dig deeper. Does the individual have any professional designations, and if so, what are they? If they are serious about that, then there is a good chance they will also take the advice they give seriously. With that said, there are some designations that should carry more water than others.

For example, I have the CERTIFIED FINANCIAL PLANNER™ certification. It took me fourteen months of Wednesday nights and Saturday morning classes, countless weekends in the library studying, and a five-hour test to pass, along with ethical and experience requirements, just to get the three letters CFP® behind my name. Some designations, while I won't call them fake, don't take much effort to obtain and don't provide the professional with much usable knowledge. My suggestion would be to Google the designation(s) and licenses of any professional you are considering working with. See what they are and mean and how long they have had them.

Now that you have found a professional with the licenses and designations you would expect, what tools do they have in their toolbox? Believe it or not, there are still companies out there that severely limit the options that their financial advisors can pick from. As the consumer, do you think it is better or worse for you that your advisor isn't limited? I will let you make up your own mind on that one. One way to find out this answer and not take their word for it (because they will all say they have a lot—and that's a relative term) is to ask for a list of the investments they can choose from. Make sure it includes all annuities, securities, and insurance options. You might be surprised by the varying length of options from one firm to another.

Another important thing to look for is their capability to use these tools. I can easily buy a table saw at Home Depot, but I might not be able to do much with it compared to a carpenter. Ask questions not just about investments, but about things a financial professional does not receive direct income from. This can include Social Security decisions, rules for Roth IRAs, what situations would Roth conversions make sense, how a trust works, the different types of education accounts (probably not for you but maybe for grandchildren), etc.

Furthermore, retirement planning should not focus solely on income. Your desire to pursue lifelong ambitions should be equally pivotal. Recognizing the purpose of the money you spend your entire building is essential. This is what triggers the Retire Boldly planning concept our team embraces. Reducing the stress of worrying about wealth management should free people to engage in the retirement lifestyle they want to pursue.

If your instincts tell you that they aren't equally knowledgeable in creating both an income plan and an action plan for your retirement, steer clear A good financial advisor, like a good carpenter, should know how to access and use many tools to your advantage. and In addition, they should know how those tools can facilitate your goals and passions as part of a bold retirement.

# *About the Author*

**Russell W. Strickler**
**Strickler Financial Group**

As the owner of Strickler Financial Group, and an Investment Adviser Representative, Russ focuses on helping clients work toward their retirement dreams through a well-thought-out strategy for retirement income.

Russ got his start in the financial services industry in 2006 as a financial advisor. He truly enjoys helping provide strategies for his clients' retirement challenges to help them make their ideal retirement a reality. Using the Retire Boldly proprietary planning process that consists of five main elements (income planning, tax planning, investment planning, legacy planning, and healthcare planning), Russ and his team are able to customize a plan for each client's unique retirement and do it in a simple, yet thorough way.

Russ holds his insurance license in the states of Michigan, Ohio, and Florida, and has passed the Series 7 and 65 securities exams. He has earned his CERTIFIED FINANCIAL PLANNER™ certification and Accredited Investment Fiduciary® designation. He has a bachelor's degree in Business Management with a minor in finance and economics from Lake Superior State University.

Russ has been published or quoted in Kiplinger's on multiple occasions.

Russ and his wife, Sarah, live in Brighton, Michigan, with their two daughters, Sophia and Olivia, and their golden retrievers, Charley and Lulu. There is nothing more important to Russ than spending time with his girls. He also enjoys visiting Higgins Lake, reading the latest about the financial industry, and watching or participating in anything related to sports. Russ is a lifetime Detroit Lions fan who believes every year is going to be their year.

**Main Office: Brighton**
10299 E. Grand River Road, Suite i
Brighton, Michigan 48116

**Satellite Office: Livonia**
17199 N. Laurel Park Drive, Suite 240
Livonia, Michigan 48152

**Telephone:** 517.618.9000
**Email:** contact@stricklerfinancial.com
**Website:** stricklerfinancial.com

**Access the QR code to visit stricklerfinancial.com.**

Made in the USA
Columbia, SC
18 March 2025